D0288022

thresholds

thresholds

How to Thrive Through Life's Transitions to Live Fearlessly and Regret-Free

SHERRE HIRSCH

HARMONY BOOKS / NEW YORK

Published in the United States by Harmony Books, an imprint of the Crown Publishing Group, a division of Random House LLC, a Penguin Random House Company, New York.
www.crownpublishing.com

Harmony Books is a registered trademark, and the Circle colophon is a trademark of Random House LLC.

Library of Congress Cataloging-in-Publication Data
Hirsch, Sherre Z.
Thresholds : how to thrive through life's transitions to live fearlessly and regret-free / Sherre Hirsch.
pages cm
1. Life change events. 2. Adjustment (Psychology) I. Title.
BF637.L53H57 2015
155.2'4—dc23
2014007579

ISBN 978-0-307-59083-1
eBook ISBN 978-0-307-59085-5

Printed in the United States of America

Jacket design: Jess Morphew
Jacket photograph: Flas100/Shutterstock

10 9 8 7 6 5 4 3 2 1

First Edition

For my husband, Jeff

Contents

Introduction

Rooms and Hallways

Whether it's our cozy bedroom, our toy-strewn family room, or our newly renovated kitchen, each of us has our favorite room in our home. But when do we ever think about the hallways? Assuming you are not living in a New York City apartment, consider how much of the space in your home consists of these passageways. We spend a lot of time traversing the hallways—and crossing the thresholds—both in our homes and in our lives.

When I talk about the thresholds of our lives, I am referring to those moments when we are in transition, those moments when we are standing between the way we were accustomed to living and a new way of thinking, feeling, and being. I'm talking about those moments when we are preparing to enter a new "room," to take the next step on the journey of our lives.

Maybe we are in the hallway because our circumstances have changed: we became engaged or our parents got divorced.

Other times it may be that something has changed within us: our job is fine but we have outgrown the work, or after five years we have become bored as a stay-at-home mother.

These moments can be disorienting and scary, sometimes painful or even heartbreaking. Other times they can be exciting, hopeful, filled with possibility. For years anthropologists have studied these hallways, these "liminal moments," a term derived from the Latin word *limen,* meaning "threshold." They have examined why we respond to them so differently when these moments are woven into the fabric of our lives. Why do some of us struggle to cross while others don't? Why do some feel paralyzing fear at any sign of change while others feel intense excitement and others immense faith? Why do some of us refuse to move forward—or worse, move backward—while others lunge ahead with gusto? Why do some burst into tears, burst into joy, or not burst at all? Why is it that we may respond one way to one transition and completely differently to another?

Is it because of our personalities? Our dispositions? Are some of us genetically better equipped to handle change? Or does it have to do with the transitions themselves? Are certain transitions just easier to make than others? Does it have to do with timing? Are there times in our lives when the stars align and times when they just don't? And most important, how can we learn to become the kind of person who embraces and thrives in those liminal moments rather than one who shrinks back fearfully?

Why Aren't All Decisions Equal?

Anthropologists have learned that there is often no direct link between our ability to make decisions and our ability to handle life changes. Some of us can decide easily whether we should drive a Ford or a Volvo or eat Italian or pan-Asian for dinner, yet when it comes to whether we should move out, move in, start a business, or get married we are completely at a loss.

Not all decisions are equal. Liminal moments are different from the other decisions of our lives. We know that our lives are constantly in flux and we need to make a ton of decisions daily to survive. But not all decisions are equal. When we are standing in a hallway, the decision feels more weighted. What we decide—unlike what we drive or what we eat for dinner—will impact the direction of our lives, perhaps profoundly. Often we don't know what is waiting for us on the other side of that threshold. And this, of course, can be terrifying.

In that moment we are scared, because the familiar rooms we came from were comfortable. There were rarely surprises. We knew what to expect. There was a feeling of security in our routines and habits. Emotionally we felt competent and prepared. Even when we were not completely happy in the room, we still knew what to do and how to do it. So now, standing at the threshold, many of us want to turn back. Most of us live by the maxim "Better the devil you know than the devil you don't." And so we prefer to stay in a familiar, unpleasant situation rather than venture across a threshold into an unfamiliar, unknown one. But once we make the decision to cross the threshold, we can begin to explore the countless new opportunities, possibilities, and experiences waiting on the other side.

When I was training to become a rabbi I incorrectly assumed that most of my congregants would come to me for advice about how to live a *Jewish* life. How do you make a home kosher? What time should I light the candles on Friday night? And once in a while they did. But most of the times they came to talk to me not when they were seeking answers about Judaism, but rather when they were facing a transition, a liminal moment. In other words, the times they came to see me were times when they were stuck in the hallways of their lives.

The reasons that they sought me out were varied. Some were dramatic, like being fired. Some were deeply painful, like losing a parent. Some were expected yet still difficult, like sending a child off to college. Some were hopeful, like getting married. Even though the details were different, the essence was the same. Everyone was talking to me about transition. They came to me to help them move from one place to another, literally and figuratively.

They were standing at the threshold between the way they were accustomed to living and some new beginning, and they were not sure what to do. Should they move forward and, if so, where and how?

When I began my career as a rabbi in a pulpit, I had many opportunities to speak intimately with my congregants at all the obvious liminal moments; people came to me to officiate their baby namings, bar mitzvahs, weddings, and funerals. In those transitional moments I often got a window into their lives that I would not have received had we met in any other context. It was a privilege to be given this trust.

Later, when I left the pulpit, I thought that my work counseling people would end. I could not have been more wrong. I was still a rabbi, but the walls of the synagogue did not confine me. My congregation became people of all religions. I became a person anyone, regardless of his or her beliefs, could come to for spiritual guidance. It was then that I decided to deepen my work and dedicate myself to helping all people cross thresholds in their personal and professional lives. And I have since discovered that while the challenges and fears of my clients are absolutely not uniquely Jewish, they are uniquely human.

Why Do We Feel That We Are Not Normal?

People came to me because they did not respond to these liminal moments the way they believed they should. They did not feel "normal." Instead of feeling worthy and proud of their promotion, they felt afraid. Instead of feeling excited about having a baby, they felt overwhelmed. Instead of feeling sadness about the death of their parent, they felt relief. So many people felt conflicted and confused by their emotions, and as a result they feared moving forward.

"Why am I feeling this way?" they would ask me. "Why am I full of self-doubt, fear, and indecision?" Right at the time when they needed to embrace their feelings, they were rejecting them. They were judging and condemning themselves. *What if I make the wrong decision? What if the future is worse than the past? Can I go back? What if I don't measure up? What if I fail? What if what I thought I wanted I don't want at all? What if I don't feel how I thought I would?* As a result they felt even worse and even more anxious about the transitions that lay ahead.

If you've ever felt this way, know that you are not abnormal. In fact, to date I have never heard someone tell me how much he or she just loves being in transition. What is there to like? Transition by nature is uncertain. Going from one place to another is daunting. Leaving our comfort zones can be terrifying. There may be some people out there who embrace transition. If you are one of those people, I did not write this book for you. I wrote this book for the rest of us.

As you may have surmised by now, this is not a book about how to make a home; rather, it is a book about how to make a life. And life, like our houses, has some great rooms. Rooms that we love and cherish. Rooms that provide us with security, happiness, and comfort. Which is exactly why forcing ourselves out of our comfort zone is not always easy. Yet it is necessary for us to move forward, to grow as human beings. The laws of entropy teach us that we cannot live in reverse. Nor can we arrive at a fixed moment in time and stay there forever. We have to move forward whether we want to or not. Søren Kierkegaard, the famous philosopher, said, "Life must be understood backwards . . . but . . . it must be lived forwards." Every one of us will have these moments. Living our life requires us to move from room to room, and once we do we are able to see that all of the vicissitudes and changes that happen in our lives are not mistakes. Rather, we can learn to embrace them as the moments that give our lives definition, meaning, and purpose.

You Are the Expert! Yes, You, Not Me

Now let me be clear. This is not a book to tell you which room is the right one to enter and how to make all the moves to get into it. I'm not here to tell you whether or not to take that promotion or make that move across the country or get that divorce. If I did that, I would be doing the very opposite of what I tell my congregants. So what *do* I tell them? I tell them, "I want you to stop looking outside of yourself for the right answers. I want you to stop turning to the so-called gurus and experts. They should not be making decisions for you. I want you to turn to you. I want you to become *your own* rabbi, minister, priest, guide, and guru." "If you meet the Buddha on the road, kill him," I like to say. It is hard to do this, I know. After all, we live in a society that encourages us to look outside of ourselves for all the answers, rather than within.

When I was pregnant with our first child (a daunting threshold if there ever was one), my friends told me that I had to immediately reserve a spot in the "Baby Coach" class. The assumption was that without a coach I could not effectively parent. Of course, being terrified of what was to come, I called to make a reservation for the fall class.

When the first day of class arrived, the first thing the coach told us, in soothing and reassuring tones, was that she had worked with hundreds of new mothers and babies. She was an expert in parenting, and with her guidance, she assured us, we too could become great parents. Yet when I walked out the door I couldn't decide whether I felt comforted or shamed by her words. On the one hand, it was comforting to know that every time my baby had a hiccup, I could call her on speed dial and she would know what to do. I did not have to worry ever again. When I had questions, she would have the answers.

On the other hand, for thousands of years mothers had parented without Baby Coaches and survived. (My mother did not have a coach and I had not turned out so bad.) What was wrong with me that I needed her? Did I lack the mothering gene? And if I called her every time my baby had a hiccup, how would I ever learn to be the perfect mother without her? Was she nothing more than a giant crutch?

A few days later I realized that I didn't *want* her to give me the answers. What I wanted to learn from her class wasn't what to do when the baby hiccuped; it was to trust in myself to figure it out. I didn't want her to teach me to become the perfect mom; I wanted her to teach me to become an *empowered* mom, one who trusted herself and her instincts. When I brought this up to her privately, she replied candidly, "If I did that, I would be out of a job."

I got it. Her entire career was thriving because we live in a society in which self-trust is not encouraged. We are expected to look outside of ourselves for answers. We are supposed to go to an expert every time the going gets rough. But the secret no one wants to tell you is that when it comes to your life, *you* are the expert. Not the Baby Coach, not the self-help guru, not the rabbi. You.

Of course, we all have teachers—people who can share suggestions, ideas, and perspectives based on their experiences and wisdom. The Jewish tradition says, "To find a teacher is to find a friend."* We are supposed to have many teachers in our lives who are true friends, people who make us better by guiding and empowering us. But they are never supposed to replace us as the architects of our own lives.

---

* Pirkei Avot 6:1.

That is why I promise you this book will not tell you how to live your life. After all, we've never met; I don't know whether you should get married, get divorced, have another child, start a business, etc. I, like you, am just trying to figure out those questions and many more each day myself.

I can't be your "expert." But I can be your teacher and your friend.

There Is No Pill or Magic Formula (I Know, Bummer)

I can't tell you which room to exit or enter, but I *can* help you change the way you *respond* to the decisions and transitions you face. I can help you look inside yourself for the answers—and help you find them. There is no secret formula or pill that will instantly transform you into someone who embraces change, thrives on it. But there are teachable skills and techniques that can help ease the passage through these hallways of your life. And if you are open to learning them, then I promise you that with practice you will no longer see these thresholds as obstacles; you will see them as opportunities. Rather than feeling fear you will feel excitement. Rather than immobilized you will be motivated. Rather than powerless you will feel powerful.

It is not going to be easy or simple. Most things of real value and meaning are not. Crossing thresholds, even anticipated ones, is complicated and challenging and can take time (after all, it takes nine months to have a baby, four years to get a degree, and at least one year to mourn a loss, just to name a few examples). And even when they are some of the most exciting moments we'll ever experience, they can still be difficult, because they activate our deepest doubts about our choices and ourselves.

The good news is that even though your feelings may be scary, crossing the threshold does not have to be. And while you might feel unprepared, unequipped, unready, in reality you already have exactly what you need. You don't need a new personality or a stroke of luck or even faith in God. (Yes, I said that!) All you need is faith in *yourself* and the willingness to take a small step forward.

We learn this from the first chapter of the Bible, the beginning of all of our stories. The story starts with God in a dark hallway. There was chaos—in Hebrew, *tohu wa bohu*—and it was ambiguous, disorienting, and confusing. God had to make a choice: go forward and create light or keep the universe cloaked in darkness. As far as we know, the universe did not come with an instruction manual. And this was God, after all. He was the boss. There was no angel or deity telling him what to do.

If God had done nothing, would light have come of its own accord? There is no way to know. All we can know is that God didn't wait around in that hallway to find out. No matter how scared or how unprepared He must have felt, He moved forward.

In the next phrase we learn that God created a *ruach*,

a wind to begin the process of creation. With that small act God went from darkness into the light. Thus the first scene of the most read book of all time tells us that when we are in turmoil, in chaos—when we are standing at a threshold and have to decide whether or not to cross—we have to go forward. We must create "our wind" to move out of the darkness.

I can help you make your wind by showing you that how you have reacted to transitions in the past is not necessarily how you have to respond in the future. You are not sentenced to repeating your old behaviors; you can break free of your patterns, once you become aware of them. With each new transition comes a choice to respond differently—and with practice you will.

Whether you are Jewish, Christian, agnostic, atheist, or something in between does not matter. This isn't about having faith in God. It's about having faith in the most important person: you.

I will help you see that the quest to find the "right" room is pointless. There is no right room. Instead I want you to learn to see *all* the rooms in front of you, around you, and within you. You may not like them all, but you will come to appreciate them because they will have shaped who you are and who you will choose to become.

I'm sure that you have had many liminal moments, and you are sure to have many more. Like God, you will be in the dark at least once, if not many times, in your life. And with each transition you will have to make a choice. What will you do? Will you go backward? Will you stay put? Or will you take action and move forward and in doing so unlock the possibility to do something truly great for yourself, for your loved ones, maybe even for the world?

The next threshold is upon you. Are you ready to cross it?

Chapter 1

Crossing Thresholds Is Scary, I Know

Nothing in this world is worth having or doing unless it means effort, pain, difficulty. . . . I have never in my life envied a human being who led an easy life. I have envied a great many people who led difficult lives and led them well.

—Theodore Roosevelt

In my sixth month of newlywedism (is that a word?), the phone rang at 6:00 a.m. Who calls at that hour? I reached over my husband and pulled the portable phone to my ear. "Yes." There was silence. Then I heard a voice. A voice that I recognized but that I had not heard in a long time. "Hello, Sherre?" "Dad, is that you?" Silence again. "Is anything wrong?" "Yes, something is very wrong."

My dad and I had always had a very tough relationship. He was not an easy father. I remember as a child seeing the movie *The Great Santini* and walking out afterward thinking the movie was a biography of my father. He was moody, volatile, and demanding. He ruled our home with an iron fist. He liked to be in control of everyone and everything. And if we fell out of line, he was quick to let us know. But my father could also be spontaneous, charismatic, and fun. He would surprise us—taking us out of school in the middle of the day to go to Disneyland or Palm Springs. But since I never knew who he was going to be, Dr. Jekyll or Mr. Hyde, it was hard for me to feel comfortable, let alone safe, around him most of the time. I spent most of my childhood living in fear of him.

By the time I graduated from high school, I was desperate for a different life. I moved across the country to go to college and declared myself financially independent. I did not want to be dependent on him anymore in any way—emotionally or financially. And the truth was that he seemed relieved.

By the time I graduated from college four years later, my parents were divorcing after twenty-nine years of marriage. Their separation was long overdue. And as they unraveled, I found myself divorcing my father as well. I began to speak to him less and less; I saw him more infrequently. I thought that at first I would miss him; but the truth was that I too was relieved.

As I made my way through my twenties, I heard from my brother that our father had moved to Washington, D.C.—just a few hours from where I was making a life for myself in New York City—but I did not make any grand efforts to see him, nor did he make any to see me. I had become so estranged from him over those years that I did not even invite him to my ordination from rabbinical school, as it would have felt like I was hosting a stranger. I knew he was hurt. He called. But by this point I was ambivalent about him and our relationship.

When I got engaged to my husband, Jeff, I debated whether to call my father to tell him. Never before had I thought about inserting him back into my life. But I had been serving as a congregational rabbi and I had counseled many people who had troubled relationships with one or both of their parents. I thought it was time that I faced my own head on.

He came to my wedding. He did not walk me down the aisle. That would have been silly. Afterward I thought that I would be proud of myself for taking the high road, but the truth was that I felt pretty neutral. I did not know him anymore. Even though he was my father, he was not a parent. Nor was he a friend. I was not sure what box to put him in.

So when the phone rang that morning, I was not prepared for his call, let alone the words that came out next. "Sherre, I have pancreatic cancer and I am going to die. I want to come to Los Angeles to be with you. I want *you* to care for me." I thought I was going to vomit right then and there. Was he kidding? I was newly married and I had barely seen him in twelve years. Plus, my brother and he had been in much closer touch over the years. I could not figure out why he would not want to go to San Francisco, where my brother lived.

I took a deep breath. I had thought that the first words out of my mouth would be "Absolutely not." But instead I heard myself say, "I will think about it, Dad," and I hung up. By this point my husband was standing beside me taking in the stunned look on my face. I explained the situation and then he asked the most reasonable question ever. "What are you going to do?"

If there ever was a threshold, a liminal moment of not knowing what to do, I was standing in the middle of it. Would I agree to care for my dying father—a man whom I'd feared and resented throughout my childhood and with whom I now had virtually zero relationship? Or would I refuse? Would I beg my brother to help me? Or would I do nothing and wait for the situation to resolve itself?

At first I was so angry. My life was finally coming together. I was married to a wonderful man. I was working as a rabbi in a job I loved. My mother was happy and lived close to me. Why was my father disturbing my happiness?

But then I realized how shortsighted I was being. My father was not doing anything *to me*. He had not asked for cancer. He was simply behaving in the way that he always had, thinking of what was best for him. And what was best for him was for me to care for him in Los Angeles. But that did not mean I had to be resentful of him. Nor did it mean I had to acquiesce to him. I was no longer his child living under his roof. I had choices. I could decide what I wanted to do. And there was no obviously wrong or right decision. I could decline his request, and it would make sense because he had not been a caring father to me. But I also could agree to his request because I wanted to care for him as I cared for so many other people in my congregation whom I had no real bond with. I could support his move to Los Angeles or I could not.

As I was deciding, I consulted my therapist, my rabbi, my husband, and my friends. Everyone had his or her opinions. "He was the worst father. Walk away and never look back." "Take care of him. You take care of everyone else." "Offer to help because you may regret not helping him later, when he dies." "Don't do anything yet; just wait and see what happens."

What everyone's advice made clear to me was that I needed to make the decision on my own, and no matter what room I chose to enter, I had no way of knowing what I would find there. If I took care of him, I might feel relieved but I might feel resentful. If I didn't, I might feel regretful or I might feel hypocritical. Either way, I might feel like I had made the wrong decision.

I was terrified. If I cared for him, was I inviting drama back into my life? Would I be able to withstand it? But if I didn't, would I regret it my entire life? Would I always look back and think I should have cared for him before he died? I spent a lot of time deliberating. I realized that I could not change my childhood. I could not change my father. But I could choose how I wanted to respond now. There was no "correct" answer. The outcome would not be perfect because there was no perfect. If my father suddenly became the father

I dreamed of in his last months of life, then I would mourn all the years we had lost. If my father continued to be the person that he had always been, then I would continue to mourn the relationship I wished we could have had.

I decided that to cross this threshold—to make the decision—I needed to learn to live with the fact that I wouldn't know what the outcome would be until it happened. But as long as I didn't cling to this narrow vision of what was *supposed* to happen, and I was open to whatever happened, then I could go forward with faith in myself that it would be okay. That I would be okay.

I called my brother; he had decided on his own to move to Los Angeles. So I decided I would agree to help care for my father, with my brother's help. Together we found him a small bungalow by the beach, and within a few weeks my father and his girlfriend moved within four miles of me and my husband.

I spent more time with my father in those next six months than I had since I was a teenager. And what happened? For one thing I found that with the medication he was taking, his personality intensified. What I had not liked before I now really despised, but the things that had been likable back then became more so. Except I did not respond the same way. I was not so reactive. I was not the little girl looking for his love and his approval. I was not relying on him emotionally and financially. I was just trying to be present for my father as he died so that he was not alone.

One day, as I wheeled him to the beach, he and I spoke

about the past. It was not how I had imagined the conversation would go, but we talked, and for some reason that I still do not understand that conversation has continued to have meaning for me over the years. A month later he died. I was not with him. About an hour before he passed, he got very agitated and very angry and threw me out of the room. I chose how to respond. I said nothing and I left. I drove back to my office. When I got there, the phone rang and my brother told me that my father had died and to please come back.

As I drove back to Santa Monica, an incredible sense of peace came over me. I had finally crossed this threshold and entered a new room. And even though it was uncomfortable and hard, it gave me closure. It gave me peace. I had had the opportunity to say good-bye. I had had the opportunity to forgive and to be forgiven. I had had the opportunity to become the person I hoped I would be in this situation. In a strange way I felt not only lucky but blessed because I had discovered I had more faith in myself than I had previously allowed myself to believe.

It's Time to Stop Using the *F* Word

Before God appeared to Moses and asked him from a burning bush to lead the people out of Egypt, Moses was living a comfortable life as a sheepherder in Midian with his wife and two sons. Then one day, with no warning, as he was leading his sheep to the far end of the wilderness, God spoke to him from a bush and asked him to free the Israelite people from Egyptian slavery and lead them into the Promised Land of Israel. (God had not spoken to anyone since the time of the patriarchs Abraham, Isaac, and Jacob almost three hundred years earlier, give or take a few.) The tradition teaches that Moses was so terrorized by the voice calling his name that he immediately hid his face behind his cloak, like a child hoping this was a nightmare that would end when he opened his eyes.

But it didn't. Soon Moses realized that God was recruiting *him* to become the leader of the people. God was asking him to give up his peaceful life in Midian and go back to Egypt where he was wanted for killing an Egyptian (read Exodus, Chapter 2, for the whole story), make what was sure to be an unwelcome request that Pharaoh free the Israelite people from slavery, and traverse the desert with 600,000 people to eventually enter Canaan, the land of milk and honey.

Moses answered the way I think most of us would. He told God no.

I imagine Moses thinking, *Why would I leave my routine, comfort, and security for this unpredictable, uncomfortable journey? I don't need this tsuris in my life.* Moses could have walked away and pretended this conversation never happened. But instead he began to rattle off reasons why he was not the right man for this charge.

First he told God that he was not qualified: *Who am I? I am eighty years old* [biblical time], *a fugitive from the law, a mere shepherder. What makes me capable?* But God disagreed and continued trying to convince Moses. *I will be with you, Moses. You will bring the people out of Egypt and together you will all worship me from this very mountain.*

At this point I imagine Moses thinking God was out of his mind. *As if. This simple plan is not feasible.* At this point God sensed Moses's total apprehension, so He suggested an alternate strategy. *Go to Pharaoh and tell him that the Israelites need three days off to pray in the wilderness and when they are done praying, you will bring them back to Pharaoh. But in truth, you will never return.*

Moses is still skeptical. *Really? You think Pharaoh is gullible enough to believe an outright lie?* Finally, having exhausted almost all of his excuses, Moses blurted out in frustration that his stutter would prevent him from being a charismatic orator and leader. God still wasn't buying it.

Moses argued with God back and forth, finding excuses and rationalizations for not going. His life was fine. In fact it was better than fine; it was good. Flaming bush or no flaming bush, God or no God, why leave this life for one that he intuitively knew would be so much harder and scarier? He would have to deal with the wrath of Pharaoh. He would have to live a nomadic life in the wilderness. There might not be enough food and water. People might die along the way. He might die trying.

Moses wasn't totally wrong. There *was* a high likelihood that many of his worst fears would become a reality.

(Many people did die en route.) And there were no promises he would succeed. (In fact, he himself never made it to the Promised Land, even though his people did.) So it makes complete sense that Moses would be hesitant to answer God's call.

When faced with a life-changing or life-upending decision or opportunity, we are not that different from Moses. We find all kinds of reasons to avoid leaving our comfort zones and crossing new thresholds because we know it will be terrifying, there will be no guarantees, and there is a real chance that some of our fears will be realized.

Like Moses, we will go to great lengths to justify avoiding change—to stay in our comfortable rooms. *My life is fine as it is. In fact, it might be better than fine; it might be good. Why should I mess with the status quo? Moving forward will take a lot of effort. It is not the right time. I am not capable. The future might be worse. Maybe others will not support me. Maybe I will hurt people I love. Maybe I will be judged or humiliated. I might make a mistake or many mistakes that will destroy everything that came before. I might want to go back and it may no longer even be an option.*

At the root of all these excuses—for Moses and for us—is the *F* word: fear. Contrary to popular opinion, fear is not always bad. In fact, it can be adaptive when there is a definite threat in front of us. (Think bear attacking.) The problem is that most of our fears are not a response to something real. Rather, most of our fears originate in our minds, in response to something we are anticipating, expecting, or imagining *might* happen.

It is not all our fault. The human tendency is to believe that all unknowns are dangerous. It is part of our evolutionary makeup. When our brains are forming, they store information about pain and danger. Where pain is actually stored is unclear. However, a 2006 study at the David Geffen School of Medicine at UCLA revealed that the same parts of the brain are activated when we experience physical pain as when we experience emotional pain, such as social rejection or a broken heart. This is one of the ways our brains reflexively prepare to protect us from situations that are potentially harmful.*

This may be why many individuals who have been abused or served in war experience posttraumatic stress disorder. The memories of the traumatic event that injured them either emotionally or physically get so deeply ingrained in their brains that they continue to relive the trauma long after the incident. Their brains don't know they are no longer in danger; their brains think they are protecting them from future harm.

---

* N. I. Eisenberger, J. M. Jarcho, M. D. Lieberman, B. D. Naliboff, "An Experimental Study of Shared Sensitivity to Physical Pain and Social Rejection," *Pain* 126 (2006): 132–38.

Trauma and Drama Are Not the Same Thing

Most of us do not have clinical posttraumatic stress disorder. But we do have varying degrees of emotional trauma—and lots of drama. This isn't a meaningless distinction. Trauma is when we were actually hurt physically or emotionally and the hurt created lasting psychological damage. Many of us have varying degrees of this. Maybe we were not abused as a child, but we were ignored or neglected. Maybe we did not witness violence, but we witnessed silence and it had a lasting impact on us. Trauma comes in many forms and its impact can last a lifetime. Drama is not the same. Drama is when something elicits in us an emotional reaction that we were not expecting. We have drama with our family over who is coming and who is not coming to Thanksgiving at Aunt Shirley's. We have drama with our mother over where to have our wedding. Though unpleasant, these are not traumatic events. They can be painful at the time but do not forever wound us emotionally.

The initial problem is that our brains tend to confuse drama and trauma. Often when we are disappointed, angry, sad, or resentful over a dramatic situation, we will claim that we have been traumatized. We will say that the experience has permanently scarred us. We react to the drama as if it were trauma. Usually we are overreacting.

But the more pressing problem is that when we have drama, we falsely project these emotions and feelings onto *future* events. Although the fears were real in the moment the drama happened, that doesn't mean we'll experience that same pain in the future. Yet our brains trick us into thinking that our past will be repeated. And this fear becomes our absolute truth and therefore our justification for not moving forward.

In my work as a counselor, I see people fall prey to this all the time. For example, Ella came to see me because she had been invited to go on a trip with her boyfriend and his family and was apprehensive—perhaps understandably, since the last time she had gone on a trip with a boyfriend, they had broken up. But when I pressed her, it turned out that her recollection of the past was not entirely accurate. Her last relationship had actually ended because the relationship had already been failing, plain and simple. The trip had just been a last-ditch effort to make it work. But she had forgotten all those details. As a result, she was falsely associating the end of her last relationship with the trip and now was using that as "evidence" to prevent her from moving into the next room—from taking this new relationship to the next level.

To make matters worse, our brains give trauma and drama top billing; as a dear therapist friend of mine says, there is no "post–good time disorder." The brain does not store past joy and then project it into the present and the future. When something good has happened in our past, we do not assume that it will happen again in our future. In fact, we actually consider our past successes anomalies and believe that we "just got lucky."

Our brains are so wired to protect ourselves from harm

that we will fixate on the one risk that did not work out, even if nine others did. As Roy Baumeister, a professor of social psychology, states, "Bad emotions, bad parents and bad feedback have more impact than good ones."* Often I hear this from people who are dating. A person will come to me and say that they will not let anyone set them up on a blind date again (even though they had gone on many good dates) because there was this "one time." All the other good dates no longer exist in their memory. The one bad date eclipses all the others.

I see this even in my own life. Often I speak to large groups of people. Afterward people come up to me with their thoughts and comments. It is always shocking to me that thirty-five people can compliment me and one person can criticize and when I get home, the first thing I report to my husband is the negative feedback. I never begin with the thirty-five positive comments, and he often has to press me to get them, because in my mind they did not exist; they were completely crowded out by the one negative comment.

Worse still is the fact that our human tendency is to distort our past memories. When our French teacher said in front of the class that we had a bad accent, it hurt very badly. We never forgot that feeling, and over time the story changed in our mind to reflect and justify the hurt we still feel. Now

---

* R. F. Baumeister, "Bad Is Stronger Than Good," *Review of General Psychology* 5 (2001).

when we tell the story, she "said," "You will never learn to speak French, let alone any foreign language. In fact, you are just plain stupid." It is not that we are trying to misrepresent the truth; rather, we are distorting it to accurately depict the pain that we felt and maybe still feel.

Ironically, this technique was adaptive when we lived in the wild. People who were able to recall past threats more readily were more likely to survive current threats. And if they intensified the threat, it only made them more hyper-aware and more safe. It is those people who survived and passed their genes on to us. After hundreds of thousands of years of evolution we are now excellent at being able to distort past threats to protect ourselves.

It is not logical, but then, most of our fears are not. They are reflexes of our brains, not thoughtful or even conscious responses. It's like how when your doctor taps the tendon under your knee, your leg flies up; our emotional responses too are almost as involuntary and sudden. When we perceive someone's words or facial expression as persecutory, our first response is to protect ourselves as if a lion were threatening us. It's an instinctive, almost animalistic reaction.

To Fear Failure Is Human

Shelly came to me because she had been invited to be a guest lecturer at a conference of film editors. At first she had refused, but they had come back and asked her to reconsider. She came to me because she knew that this was a great opportunity to advance in her field and make some extra money that she needed, but she was full of fear. What if she performed badly? What if she got stage fright? What if "they" discovered that she was not who they thought she was? (Isn't it funny how there is always the "they," the nameless people whom we refer to when trying to justify our fears? Who were "they" exactly in this case? The conference organizers? The attendees? Her colleagues? Her parents? Who is actually that committee in our head that we give tremendous authority to?) Shelly's mind was so filled with self-doubt and self-destructive thoughts that she could not entertain the possibility that she had been invited because of her genuine ability. She could not even begin to think that she would possibly be successful. She was absolutely sure that she would be humiliated and would never work again.

To counsel Shelly I first had to help her understand that she was letting herself be controlled by her fears. Yes, her fear of what could happen was real; contained within our fears are often kernels of real possibilities of disappointment. All those things could actually happen. She could get stage fright. She might stutter, say something she would regret, quote misinformation. Someone might know more than she did and even correct her publicly. She could fail. And nothing I could say to her would remove that reality. *But* what she neglected to realize was that there were also real possibilities of rewards. She could discover she had a gift for speaking. She could be excellent. She could even have fun and be invited back again.

What Shelly had failed to do was balance her negative "what if's" with positive ones. It seems obvious that when we make a list of what could happen there should be two columns, the negative and the positive. But we rarely make the list at all. We are so certain that our fears are facts that we forget our emotional burden of proof. To address our fears honestly we have to learn to balance our evidence with the counterevidence. In our careers, and even more so in our relationships, we often get trapped in a room because we wrongly assume our worst fears will come true and we don't even bother with the evidence to the contrary.

The other mistake Shelly made was overestimating the consequences of her fears coming true. For her, giving a poor speech would be evidence of so much more than simply having made a poor speech; it would be evidence that the entire enterprise was a mistake: giving the talk, accepting the invitation, working as a film editor. She feared that this one act would put her entire self-worth at risk. She would be destroyed not only professionally but also personally and emotionally. She would see *herself* as a mistake.

On the surface, we often do not cross thresholds because we are afraid of what failure might look like. We don't want to be humiliated. But I think that reason only scratches the surface of the truth. The core reality is that we are afraid a failure will confirm our worst fears that being here in this world is a mistake, that we are not "someone." We do not necessarily need to be famous or rich or powerful, but we need to know that we have a place in this world. That we can positively impact those around us. That our being here actually matters.

The irony is that our fear of being a mistake is so powerful that it prevents us from taking risks to change our world—from doing the very things that would prove to ourselves and to others that we are anything but a mistake.

I am often surprised how many people tell me they avoid taking risks, *even when the last risk they took turned out great*. You would think that if your past experience proved successful—the risk was completely worth it—then of course it would inspire you to take another. But this is so often not the case.

For example, a friend of mine wrote a book that became a best seller. She had never imagined that it would be read and bought by so many people. She was thrilled. Her agent, her publisher, and her audience could not wait to read her second book. But she did not want to write it. She was afraid of the sophomore slump.

The sophomore slump, also known as the sophomore jinx, does not refer only to our years in college. It refers to any time in our lives when we fear that the second (or "sophomore") effort will not live up to the first one. It is when we become unable to move forward because we fear that we can never repeat our original success.

We have valid reasons to fear the sophomore slump. Every day in the media we hear about athletes, musicians, and the like who had one tremendous success that they could never live up to again. *Her first album went to the top of the charts, but the second did not even break the top one hundred. In his first season he broke the record, but he was benched most of the second year. The original movie was amazing, but the sequel/prequel did not even come close.*

But would you rather be known as a one-hit wonder who knocked it out of the park the one and only time you tried or as someone who succeeded and then kept challenging herself to reach new levels of greatness?

It follows that if we are scared to move forward when we have had past success, moving forward when we have had disappointment and failure in the past is even *more* daunting. What if we repeat the same mistakes?

After thirteen years of marriage, two kids, and therapy, Danny and Alexa divorced. For a while they had both tried everything to make their marriage work. Eventually they stopped trying. Alexa had an affair with a man from work and Danny was devastated. He perceived her straying as evidence that he had failed her as a husband. They proceeded to divorce and it was messy. They fought over custody and money. Eventually they went their separate ways.

Years later, Alexa remarried and Danny was dating a lovely woman whom his children liked. Even his ex-wife was happy that he was moving on. Danny's girlfriend wanted to marry him, but he was terrified. He had failed once before as a husband; what if he failed again? What if she too had an affair? What if their marriage also ended in divorce? Danny was not naive. He did not believe the failure of his first marriage had been solely his fault. He knew intellectually that it had ended for many reasons. But emotionally he could not shake the fear that this second marriage would end the same way. Then would he label himself or would others perceive him as the guy whom women leave? Would he see himself as a loser because he "failed" not once but twice? Would it cause him to give up on love completely?

We are often scared to cross the threshold because we have "failed" in the past and we are afraid of failing again. However, it is very unlikely that we will fail again and even less likely that we will fail again in the same way. As Samuel Beckett said, "Try again. Fail again. Fail better."* You may fail, but the next time you will fail better because you learned from past mistakes. And if you confront your fear of repeating the same mistakes, eventually you will find success, although it may look different from what you anticipated.

* Samuel Beckett, *Worstward Ho* (New York: Grove Press, 1984).

If You Think You Are a Fraud, You Are Not Alone; Maya Angelou Did Too

For years psychologists have studied the reflex responses of our brains—the "fight or flight" system—trying to understand why, when we sense any kind of danger, real or imagined, we react to defend ourselves, whether doing so is rational or not. Another manifestation of this is our tendency to feel, regardless of our success or position in life, that we are a fraud. This "impostor syndrome" causes us to convince ourselves that we are faking it and do not deserve our success, despite evidence of real competence. We tell ourselves our success was due not to our talent or our efforts but to some other reason outside of us, like timing or luck.

Research done in the 1980s found that two out of five successful people considered themselves frauds, and other studies have found that 70 percent of all people feel like impostors at one time or another. Even the most celebrated authors and actors feel these fears. Maya Angelou once said, "I have written eleven books, but each time I think, 'Uh oh, they're going to find out now. I've run a game on everybody, and they're going to find me out.' "

On the one hand, this tendency can have the positive effect of keeping a person humble and hardworking. On the other hand, though, it can result in the kinds of paralyzing fears that keep us from moving into the next room. If we constantly believe that we are not competent, then we will tend to become risk averse. Why would I put myself out there if my secret that I have scammed you will be uncovered? I would be a fool not only in your eyes but also in my own. Then I would lose my dignity, stature, and reputation. Without those I would consider myself worthless. Better to lie low, stay in my comfort zone.

Plus, when we are consumed with running the day-to-day operations of our families and our lives, we don't make the time—or even have the desire—to deeply think about these life questions. Do we really want to contemplate our existence and our task in this world? Do we really have time to stop and think about how much power and control we have in our world to change it?

No. But when we fail to challenge our fears, this is precisely how they are reinforced, and this is in turn precisely how, like Moses, we justify not taking a risk to cross a new threshold.

Deep inside, each one of us knows that we have no control of others or the workings of the world, and it scares the bejesus out of us. It is why we spend many of our waking hours making intricate routines, schedules, and lists so that the next moment is predictable. If I know where I have to be on the Tuesday after next and what I will be doing next summer, then I don't have to think about how little control I have. I can just disconnect. I can turn off that channel of fear. I can pretend that I am in control when in fact I am really just on autopilot.

But liminal moments force us to think about these questions. Because as hard as we try to push them away in our regular lives, when we are standing at a threshold these questions are shoved in our faces and we cannot escape them.

To Fear Loss of Control Is Also Human

When Irwin, a congregant of mine, was dying of terminal cancer, his son called and said that his father was asking for me. Even though I knew Irwin, we had never had an intimate conversation. He was not a guy who asked for help, certainly not the type to consult with a rabbi. He was a CEO in every aspect of his life. He was in charge of his business and his family. He was in control of his entire world. But now, as the cancer was taking over, he was forced to come face to face with the fact that he was anything but.

He had a lot of questions for me when I arrived at his bedside. Would he go to heaven? Would he be forgiven for his missteps? Would he be reunited with his parents? Would his family be okay? The questions kept coming. Had he made a difference in this world? What was his purpose?

I had no answers to these questions. So I asked him a question instead. (Note: Always a good strategy: When you don't know, ask.) I was not trying to be callous, but I wanted to know. "Irwin, did you ever think about all these questions before you got cancer?" I thought I knew the answer. Given what I knew about his personality, I thought he would say definitively no. But instead he said, "Of course I did, but every time I pushed them aside. I did not want to think about how little control I had in the world because then I might get cancer and spend my time worrying about how I would handle dying rather than living."

Many of us believe, as Irwin did, that if we thought about how little control we actually have, our fears would paralyze us. We would not want to wake up in the morning. We would be so depressed and despondent that we would not ever want to move forward and take risks. We would not want to find connections, be good, and better the world. And of course we would not want to leave the rooms we are comfortable in. Irwin had spent his life pushing away all these feelings, until this moment, when he had no other choice but to confront them.

But in these moments when we are about to cross a new threshold, and even more so when we are about to cross the *final* threshold, we can no longer turn them off. The fears are wild and uncontained. They rage in our minds. And we can't ignore them; we have to address them. And they are terrifying.

To Fear Hurting Those Whom We Love Is Divine

Irwin, like so many of us, was not only afraid for himself but was also deeply afraid for the people he was leaving behind. When he left this world, their lives would be radically changed. And he was worried about how they would manage. But it is not only when we are at death's door that we worry about how our decision to move to the next room will affect those around us. We worry about it in good times and neutral ones as well.

Most of us do not live in isolation. Our lives are deeply intertwined with others'. Maybe it is obvious. We are part of a big family and we have children and parents who depend on us. Or we are in a position in which a lot of people rely on us for their livelihood or success. But many times our impact on others is not so apparent. Many of us live seemingly private lives. Maybe we live alone. We don't have a lot of friends. We are only "seen" by a small few. But whether you are in a huge network or not, when you make a move, it will have a ripple effect.

In life it is overwhelming to think about how our decisions will impact others. We may fear that crossing a threshold will cause people we love to suffer. If we decide to move across the country, we worry about the effect on the friends and family we leave behind. If we get a divorce, we worry about how it will impact our young child. This is certainly true when someone is dying. Every person I know who is aware that their time is limited on this earth spends more time worrying about those they leave behind than about what lies ahead for them. But it is not just in death and dying that people worry. All the time, even in the most joyful moments, people worry about the impact of their actions on others.

In good times or bad, the thought of causing pain to people we love and respect is awful. But we have to put aside those fears and move ahead regardless.

Ellen and Rick are a "typical" middle-class couple who both work. They own their house and they have family nearby. When they had their first child, they were in bliss. They loved Ethan so much. After a few years, everyone was asking them if they were going to take the next step and expand their family. And while they wanted to, they had so many fears. How would a second child affect the first? How would it impact their marriage? What effect would it have on their parents, already the part-time caretakers? Would they still help, or would it be too much for them? How would it affect Ellen and Rick's own lifestyle? Would one of them have to stay home or work longer hours? Would they have to move? Would they still have time to go out with their friends? Their fears were endless.

What made it even worse for them was that they felt that they could not discuss their concerns with their friends and family, for fear of being judged. So many of their friends were having a hard time getting pregnant. To their ears Rick and Ellen would sound whiny and ungrateful. Other friends who had more than one child would see their concerns as silly and trivial. Their parents might have their own agenda and try to sway them one way or the other. So ironically, their fears were intensified by their fear of how others were going to perceive their fears. Would they be ridiculed or judged? Would they be encouraged and supported? These concerns only made the decision more daunting.

When they came to see me, I sensed that they wanted to have another child and had sought me out hoping I would assuage their fears (after all, I had four children!). This didn't particularly surprise me; human nature is to seek advice from people who will confirm what we wish to hear. So they were almost offended when I did not tell them, "Don't worry. Have more kids." Instead I told them that I could not alleviate their fears. I did not have the power to see into the future. I was not a fortune-teller.

They were even less impressed when I went on to tell them that, in fact, many of their fears probably *would* become reality. Ethan might indeed be upset and have a hard time dealing with no longer being the center of attention. Their parents might very well not want to babysit. Their lifestyle would probably change. But that reality was not everything. They would also have many unexpected blessings and joys that they could not yet imagine.

So about a year later, when I got a call asking me to do the bris for their second son, I asked them what had made them take the plunge. Rick said simply, "I don't want to look back in my life and say that I let fear be the most deciding factor of the important decisions of my life."

Wiser words were never uttered.

Yet a full decade later, Emily was on the brink of a new threshold, and fear reared its ugly head again. This time she came to talk to me because she was terribly conflicted about whether to go back to work. Before she had her children, she had worked in public relations. She had had a nice income, a good title, and a sense of pride and accomplishment. When her first child was born, she had decided to stay home as a full-time mother. Then she had a second child and then a third. After about ten years, once her three children were all in school full time, she was anxious to return to the working world. But when she brought it up to her family, they were far from supportive. Who would pack their lunches each day? Drive carpool? Pick up the dry cleaning? Who would make dinner and do their laundry? She was devastated because she wanted to move forward in her professional life but she also wanted her family's full support.

Now her fear of returning to the working world was compounded by her fear of disappointing her family. She had always been there for them. That was her job and she did it well. She could not imagine living with the feeling that she was not caring for them in the way *they* thought she should. It was the reason she was leaning toward staying in her role as a stay-at-home mother even though it was not at all what she wanted.

I asked her if she could live with the discomfort of disappointing her family. She said she could only if she knew that their disappointment would end at a given time. I empathized. It is easier metaphorically to run a race with a finish line than to go on a long run with no end point. With an ending in sight, it's easier to tell ourselves we can endure and push through the pain. Without one, we believe that the pain will never end.

I suggested that she should decide how long they were reasonably entitled to be angry with her if she went back to work. She laughed. I was not sure if it was because she thought my question was ridiculous or because she realized how silly it would be to let fear of their anger determine whether she moved forward in her professional life. She promptly thanked me and left.

A few months later I ran into her at afternoon carpool. Given that carpool is at 3:00 p.m.—a time when most employed people are at work—I first thought this was a sign that she had dismissed my advice and let fear get the better of her after all.

How wrong and arrogant I was to make this assumption. She *had* gone back to work. At first her family was upset. But after about three weeks, they found a new routine and got over their disappointment that from now on she would be home much less. But then she realized that she missed them too much and really did not *want* to work full time. In the end, she was able to arrange a part-time situation that made everyone much happier—including her.

You Are Stronger Than You Think

The key to moving through a threshold is to remind ourselves that even if our fears *do* come true, it will never be as bad as we think it will be. All of us tend to underestimate our coping capabilities. We believe that we cannot survive the uncomfortable feelings that may come with our decision. But the truth is, we are much stronger and more resilient than we give ourselves credit for.

"Resilience" seems to be the new buzzword in the psychological community. For years it was believed that resilience was an extraordinary trait that only a few of us possessed. But now we have discovered that resilience is not a trait just the lucky few can develop; rather, it is ingrained in all of us. The result is that most of us can cope with far more unknowns and challenges than we think.

George Bonanno stunned the science world when he published his book, *The Other Side of Sadness*. For years most everyone had subscribed to Elisabeth Kübler-Ross's theory of grieving, which says that when a loved one dies, we universally experience five stages of grief (denial, anger, depression, bargaining, and acceptance). Then Bonanno and others pointed out that there was a flaw in her method: she had studied the people who were dying, not the people who were left to pick up the pieces after the one they loved passed away. Bonanno decided to study the ones who had to mourn. And what he found was that we don't uniformly experience the stages of grief that the Kübler-Ross hypothesis suggests. Our experiences of grieving are as unique as our identities. But what we do share is the innate ability to cope and be resilient. To pick up the pieces, rebuild, and go on. Most of us, Bonanno found, are actually far better at coping than we think. We will be sad, maybe even devastated, by our loss, but we will go on and we will thrive.

I have been reminded of this truth again and again by the people I counsel in my professional life. I have met so many people who have suffered terrible losses and believed without a doubt that they could not go on. They swore that they would not survive, and if they did, that they would never smile or laugh or love again. But they did.

I felt a special connection with one of them, Miles, the minute he walked through my door and told me this story. He was seventy years old when the love of his life died suddenly. He had never imagined his life without her. They had been together since they were fourteen, and they were soul mates. He had never imagined for a moment that he would be alone; he had always been sure that he would die first. Without her, he was convinced that life was not worth living. He had even contemplated suicide so that he could "be with her," but luckily, as he said, he "lacked the courage." So he decided he would come to synagogue each week and pray that God would take him. It was heartbreaking.

On one of those Saturdays, as he was praying to die, a woman sitting behind him tapped him on the shoulder. She was in her forties and pretty. She explained that her mother was widowed and she would like to introduce the two of them. At first he politely declined. But she was persistent. Week after week she asked, until he finally agreed to take her mother out for coffee. He told me it was not love at first sight when he met Sylvia, as that only happens "once in a lifetime" and he had already had his one true love. But it was definitely *like* at first sight. The more time they spent together, the more he enjoyed her company, and she his. After two years of dating, he sat in my office asking me to officiate at their wedding, in which their grandchildren would serve as the best boys and girls.

I will never forget standing under the chuppah, looking at Miles gazing at Sylvia as she came down the aisle in her white lace floor-length wedding gown. I had never seen a man who just two years earlier had wanted nothing more in the world than to die showing so much love and joy in his face. That moment confirmed to me that every one of us has far more resilience within us than we can even fathom.

Are You Afraid That You Are Not Worth It?

I told Miles's story to Julie, a woman who was having trouble breaking off an engagement to Charles, a man she clearly didn't love (the way she spoke about him, I might have thought he was her dog, not her fiancé). But at thirty-three she did not want to cross that threshold (indeed, a relationship that is not working can often be the hardest room to leave). What if Charlie was her last chance for true love? What if she never got married? What if she came to regret leaving him? What if she was just spooking herself? Julie was so paralyzed by the fear that she was unworthy of something better, it was preventing her from doing anything at all.

I told Julie that she *would* find love again, and it would not be when she was eighty! But first she had to address her fear of uncertainty. The other point that I shared with Julie was that her inaction, her "not doing anything," *was* actually doing something. She could not stop time. The wedding day would eventually come. If she continued to stay in that room she did not want to be in, she would end up married to someone she had real ambivalence about marrying. She would be tacitly accepting less than what she believed she deserved, something other than what she really wanted. She would be settling.

We've all had experiences of "settling" out of fear of being somehow undeserving in our relationships, our careers, or other aspects of our lives. We try to prove to ourselves we are not settling by claiming, "If it ain't broke, don't fix it." Every time I hear this phrase, I think of a blinking yellow light. It tells me that even though something does not look obviously broken on the outside, it probably has a significant but not readily visible fracture.

Julie's engagement did not look broken. He was a good guy. He loved her. Their families were compatible. Their lifestyles were in sync. But in her heart she did not want to marry him. And because she did not have an apparent reason to justify her position, owning the decision to walk away was even more daunting. Julie believed that it was safer for her to stay put and to settle.

In this Julie is not the exception; many of us behave this way, and not just in our romantic lives. I met Isabelle years ago when I walked into her travel agency. (Remember those?) I sat down assuming we were going to have a simple exchange. I would tell her where I wanted to go, she would tell me the best way to get there, and then she would issue the tickets and I would leave. This is not what happened.

Before I continue, you should know that I pride myself on being a good listener. I discovered this when I was eleven years old and called the 411 operator to ask for the number of our local library. Forty-five minutes later I was still on the phone with Lydia, the operator from Georgia, listening to her talk about how her husband had left her and how she was having trouble coping with raising two children alone. The point is, people have always confided in me, so it was not so unusual when Isabelle the travel agent began telling me that she had worked this job for eighteen years—since the very day after she finished high school. It paid the bills but she had been given a raise only twice. Her boss was a jerk. He criticized her and berated her. She was bored most of the time. And the travel industry was becoming obsolete. By all reasonable standards, these were very good arguments for quitting. But then she surprised me by saying that she was never going to leave this job. She was going to stay put as long as they would let her. (As I sat listening to her, I had an image of her glued to her seat while a wrecking ball destroyed the building around her.)

She believed that this life, with this terrible boss and monotony, was all she deserved. She did not have a "big" education. She was not skilled at other trades. But did that mean she deserved to be undervalued, underpaid, and underappreciated? To be criticized harshly by an abusive boss? She apparently thought so.

But when I pressed her, I discovered she *did* want more. She wanted to be in an environment where she was appreciated and respected. She wanted to grow her skills in social media and begin to do her job in more creative new ways. But I could tell her fear of uncertainty, combined with her feelings of low self-worth, kept her stuck in that hallway. She had settled for what she thought she deserved, not what would possibly make her happy.

I am not saying that every time you choose not to move forward into the next room you are settling. There are times in our lives when we are content in our rooms. We are far from suffering. We are satisfied and even happy. It is absolutely okay to want exactly what you have and to stay in that room for a while. *But you can't stay there forever.* Albert Einstein said, "A ship is always safe at the shore—but that is not what it is built for." We can stay on the shore and we will be safe for now, but if we stay there forever, we will never go to new places and have new experiences.

Sherre Hirsch

Pain Does Not Have to Be the Touchstone

We often hear that pain is the impetus to grow. And many of us wait until the pain is intolerable to begin to contemplate changing our status quo. But why should we wait until we are in pain to make a change? Maybe when we are satisfied and content is exactly when we should consider entering a new room. Maybe when we are fulfilled in our job is when we should think about making a move up the career ladder. Maybe when we are happy in our marriage is when we should think about having a child. Maybe when we are comfortable dating is the time to think about getting engaged. Maybe when we are happy, and not in pain, is the right time to take a risk and move forward, instead of waiting until we are forced to. Maybe we should leave the shore and sail when the waters are calm instead of waiting for the storm.

It is a reality that crossing new thresholds is scary. But fear is not our fault, nor is it our fate. We have the ability to override our reflexes, recognize our fears, and even face them, but we have to make a decision. Will we let our fears hold us back? Will our fears dictate our life story? The amazing thing about life is that it has an infinite number of rooms; it holds endless possibilities for joy, countless opportunities for success and fulfillment. The path in front of us may not always be easy, but is that really a good enough reason not to forge ahead and seize those possibilities?

Chapter 2

Faith in God Is Not Required

As soon as you trust yourself, you will know how to live.

—Johann Wolfgang von Goethe, *Faust*

There, I said it. I believe in God—most of the time. But you don't have to. In fact, I know a lot of you don't. And you may never. Finding faith in God is difficult for even the most pious. Faith in God is not a requirement for living a full and happy life. I know that this must sound surprising coming from a rabbi. Most people think that my job is to *convince* them to believe in God. But it is not.

Whom or what you believe in is up to you. The Hebrew word for "to pray" is *l'hitpallel.* It is in the reflexive voice, which means that when you pray, you pray to yourself. With this small grammatical distinction the Jewish language is telling us an important truth about our lives: faith begins with you.

Even Sigmund Freud, who for most of his life argued against God and religion, praised Judaism's focus on turning inward. He claimed, "To live well, the modern individual must learn to understand himself in all his singularity. He must be able to pause and consider his character, his desires, his inhibitions and values, his inner contradictions."*

So crossing the thresholds of your life requires you to believe, but not necessarily in God. Whatever religion you practice or don't practice, whatever ideology you espouse or don't, really does not matter. What matters is whether you believe in you.

We typically use the word "faith" when discussing our religious beliefs, but faith is not limited to religion. To have faith means merely to trust that you are exactly where you are supposed to be in this moment because all the experiences of your life together have led you here. This means that all experiences that came before this moment—the great, the difficult, and the mediocre—did not exist independently of one another. Rather, they were shaped, defined, and created *because* of one another.

Therefore, when you are faced with a difficult choice, scary transition, or daunting threshold in your life, finding the courage to move forward doesn't require faith in God or some particular organization; it simply requires that you have faith in yourself.

---

* Mark Edmundson, "Defender of Faith?" *New York Times Magazine* (September 9, 2007).

All our lives have been filled with moments of greatness, difficulty, and the mundane—sometimes all three woven together. When you have faith, you realize that you have the ability to decide how to respond to this moment and, in doing so, choose the life you want to live.

Some of you may say that what I am describing as faith is just self-confidence. But it is not. Our confidence in ourselves can be easily shattered when a situation or another individual turns out differently from what we expected or wanted. But when we have faith, even when things don't turn out as we planned, we stay in the game. We still continue to cross the thresholds in front of us because we trust in the choices that we have made and will continue to make.

This is not to say that if you simply have faith, hard choices will automatically become easy. You will not suddenly welcome all liminal moments—especially the scary ones—with open arms. Rather, it means that you will be able to face your fears rather than run from them. You will know that when you make the decision to cross the threshold into a new room, whether it turns out totally as you expected, nothing like what you expected, or somewhere in between, you won't collapse.

Why Do We Lack Faith in Ourselves?

Humans in general inherently struggle to believe in themselves. This is not so surprising when you consider that each of us comes into this world relying on the care of others; our very survival as babies and then children (and even as adolescents and adults) depends on it. According to Roderick Kramer, the William R. Kimball Professor of Organizational Behavior at Stanford Business School who has studied trust for over thirty years, we are genetically hardwired to let other people care for us from day one. This is the reason babies in their very first months of life will giggle and smile and make eye contact with those around them; they are looking to engage people to care for them. We are born to be reliant on others.

Moreover, our initial life experiences—being cared for by our parents—do not teach us from the get-go to be self-reliant. As we mature, our life experiences can enhance or erode our trust and faith in ourselves. If we feel as we grow that others around us trust us and we see ourselves becoming exactly whom we believe we were meant to be, our faith in ourselves grows. But many of us are not raised in these perfect conditions.

Instead, many of us learned directly or indirectly that life's struggles are not challenges or adventures to be embraced but rather dangers to be avoided at all costs. So when a challenge or hardship surfaces, we don't trust in our ability to overcome or even grow from it—instead, we run.

Sometimes we can point to a person or an incident that led us to question our faith in ourselves. Maybe a parent or a teacher criticized us. Maybe a peer bullied or teased us.

Maybe our parents acted in ways that subtly implied they did not always trust us. In some cases for a small few of us, our anger and hurt inspired us to work harder to prove that person wrong, but for most of us, this was unfortunately not the case. Consciously or not, we internalized these messages, and from that point on we began to tell ourselves, *I am not _____ (athletic, smart, powerful, successful, worthy, competent, loving, kind . . .).* (You fill in the blank.)

Maddie, for example, was raised by a very demanding, critical mother, and she spent most of her childhood trying to please her. Everything her mother wanted her to do she committed to with a vengeance: school, sports, and violin. She didn't even enjoy many of these activities, but she was desperate for her mother's approval. She went to a top-tier college and then graduated at the top of her law-school class, yet with every accomplishment her mother pointed out what she *hadn't* accomplished rather than what she had. When she landed a great job, her mother reminded her she didn't have a husband. When she was married with children, she was told she did not parent correctly. Nothing she did ever seemed good enough.

When I met Maddie at forty-two, she was still trying to gain her mother's approval. After all these years, her mother's word was her gospel; she truly believed that she would never be enough. It's understandable that she had no faith in herself; her decisions and choices had been questioned her entire life!

Sometimes there's no single person or incident that causes us to lose our faith in ourselves; it happens more gradually over a series of situations or relationships in our lives that make us continually question our worth. Maybe we did not feel loved as a child. Maybe we felt diminished, discarded, or insignificant. Maybe our sibling always shined brighter than we did. Maybe we never felt that our parents believed in us. The details of such experiences are different for each of us. But what is the same for all of us is that these messages stick with us long after those situations are over and these people gone from our lives. Even after the memory of the event itself fades, its impact remains.

Slowly, as our faith in ourselves declines, we begin to think of our life as a series of "rules"—this is what I can and cannot do. This is what I *should* and should not do. After all, if we've been told over and over that we are no good at something, why even bother trying? Thus we begin to edit our experiences because we begin to believe that we actually are incapable.

When my mother was working in retail, she once had to take a math test, presumably to make sure that she could handle money. For reasons I did not understand, she was stricken with fear—she even considered quitting her job because of it. My mother was an intelligent woman and quite competent at managing money; after all, she was a single parent and handled all of our bills. But every time I sat down to help her study, she froze like a deer in headlights. Finally I learned why. In grammar school in her small town, her math teacher had repeatedly told her she was incompetent at math. Then when she got to college, she had been bombarded with messages that "girls are not good at math." When she married, her husband told her repeatedly that she was stupid, especially with numbers. Over time she came to truly believe that she was unable to do math, even though her life experience proved otherwise. Those messages had become firmly implanted in her mind and they were haunting her and killing her faith all these years later.

What makes matters worse is how stubbornly we cling to those negative messages that erode our faith, how even when a person or incident contradicts those beliefs, we call them flukes. To us they are not proof that the message could actually be faulty or blatantly wrong. Rather, we consider them anomalies that we should discard from our memories. And discard them we do. Ideally those "flukes" should remind or confirm to us that "our limits" may not be accurate. They should be proof that we have greater potential and possibility than what we have been led to believe. But for most of us this is not how our brain works.

So what can we do?

Practice Does Not Make Perfect

Luckily, there is good news. You don't have to be helpless against the tricks your subconscious mind plays on you. These messages don't *have* to stick around forever. Yes, you will be standing in front of many more intimidating thresholds and you will have to make many more difficult decisions over the course of your life. And when you do, these messages will rear their ugly heads and remind you that you should be of little faith. But you don't have to listen to them. You can rebuild your faith in yourself if you have lost it. You can find your faith if you think you never had it. You can trust yourself again. Your faith in you is not permanently destroyed, even if you are convinced that it is. But finding that faith—and, more important, keeping it—takes practice.

Let's face it, practice sucks. I hated practicing piano, like almost every other kid in America. And I complained incessantly. I remember my teacher saying over and over, "Practice makes perfect," and all I wanted to do was vomit. Playing those bars again and again was constantly frustrating because I was convinced my piano teacher was a liar: my piano playing never sounded close to good, let alone perfect.

It was not until I started doing yoga thirteen years ago that I relearned what it really means to practice. Turns out my piano teacher was wrong after all. Practice, I learned, isn't about achieving perfection. You see, when we practice yoga we are not trying to master the pose. The goal is not to perform it perfectly. Rather, each time we practice an asana (a pose), it is the errors that teach us how to become a yogi. In yoga as in life, it's the mistakes that lead us to personal growth.

In yoga our mistakes are not opportunities to beat ourselves up. They are not supposed to make us think, *I need to practice more. I need to practice better next time.* In fact, saying that is detrimental to your practice because it takes you out of the present. The true end goal in yoga is not to become a perfect yogi; it is to become a person who is awake and present in his or her life.

This is the opposite of what I was taught growing up. The goal then was to practice the instrument, the sport, or the skill again and again until it was perfect. It was assumed that as long as I practiced I could achieve any goal.

What yoga has taught me—and what findings in neuroscience have now confirmed—is that doing something again and again will not make it perfect, but it will make it less difficult. That's because, as science has found, the pathways in our brains function like muscles. The more we exercise them, the stronger they become. This is why if you practice a backhand in tennis wrong over and over again, you will eventually have perfected a terrible backhand. And this is also why when we repeat the negative messages in our brains without correcting them, over time they become our reflexive response. Scientists call this "going back brain" because we are not using our thinking brain. Rather, we are switching to autopilot.

Mistakes are the signposts that tell us we need to reflect upon what we are thinking or doing; in other words, they turn our "going back brain" off. This way, the next time that same situation is upon us, we stop and think about what we are doing, rather than going on autopilot. Through this kind of practice, errors stop being proof of what we are *not* capable of; instead they become opportunities to pause and remind ourselves what we *are* capable of.

When I met Ellie, I realized quickly that she had been practicing all wrong. Every date she went on that did not work out confirmed to her what she believed about herself: that she was not worthy of a relationship. And to her autopilot brain, with each successive date, that truth became more and more manifest. Soon it was as though she walked into each date with a sign on her head that said, "Don't date me; I am not worth it."

I counseled her to see her future dates differently. I encouraged her to practice dating like practicing yoga, not like practicing the piano. The goal of each of them was not to find the man of her dreams. Each one was not to confirm or discount her worthiness of a relationship. Each one was an opportunity to get to know someone new and to learn more about how she felt about herself with different people. Now each "error" was information that would help her approach the next one and the next one.

This forced her to stop and really think objectively about what had happened on her dates, and when she did, she realized that the guy who texted during dinner was too distracted, and she needed someone more present. The guy who was so crazy good-looking made her nervous and she acted silly. The guy who talked the entire time about his mother scared her. She came to see that the reason these dates hadn't worked out was simply that these guys weren't right for her, not that she was unlovable or unworthy.

As we talked, I could see her breathe a sigh of relief. She told me that this practice took the pressure off dating. Before, she had looked at each date as a test, and when it did not work out, she saw it as a failure. But now, as she approached dating with this newfound faith in herself, she started to see each date as an opportunity to learn about herself and what she wanted in a relationship, rather than to prove how relationship incapable she was.

When any new experience or "room" in our house—a new date, a new relationship, a new city, a new job—does not turn out exactly as we expected (and what does?), it is tempting to deem it a failure. Over time those "failures" chip away at our faith until we believe *we* are a failure.

But what if instead we learned to look at that experience as practice—opportunities to pause, turn off our autopilot, and silence those negative messages echoing in our heads? What if we instead used those experiences as a chance to remind ourselves of all the times we've *succeeded* and to see those successes not as flukes but as evidence that we are *not* failures—whether at our jobs or in our relationships or at math or anything else?

What Are We Saying to Ourselves?

If we want to discover our faith or find it anew, we must begin by rephrasing what we say to ourselves. When we practice rewriting these internal messages, the words we use matter. Words, after all, are tremendously powerful. The Jewish tradition has been passed down through generations via words; these words have transmitted centuries' worth of knowledge and wisdom long after the people who uttered them have died. As kids we often heard the playground mantra "Sticks and stones may break my bones, but words will never hurt me." This couldn't be further from the truth. In reality it is always the words that hurt the most, long after the physical bruise is healed.

I see people use words to make great exaggerations out of individual episodes. All the time I hear mothers say, "I am a terrible mother because I lost it with my kids yesterday." More accurate would be "I was having a hard day; I was frustrated and tired and lost my temper." Notice the difference: the second is a description of what happened rather than a statement about her sense of self. The words we use to interpret our reality matter.

So how do we better phrase and frame the past experiences of our lives? How can we learn to describe them accurately rather than turn them into gross exaggerations about our self-worth? How can we use them as practice to help us navigate the next threshold differently? How can we use them to craft and strengthen our faith rather than to demolish it?

. . .

A rare few of us can quickly ascertain when we are putting ourselves down or framing a situation inaccurately, but unfortunately most of us can't. Many of us have unconsciously reinforced negative statements about ourselves for so long that we don't even identify them as such. They've become so familiar to us that we think they are accurate descriptions of who we are.

Wendy, for example, heard for years that she was fat. As a child she was never more than ten pounds heavier than the average kid, but nonetheless her peers repeatedly mocked her. She was called names and picked last for sports teams. Over time she began to see herself as a "fat girl." As an adult, though barely even overweight, she would often describe herself in this way and people would look at her with confusion. In their eyes and by medical standards, she was normal sized. Yet she didn't even realize her words were false because she had been repeating them for so many years.

If you are like Wendy and not able to recognize the (false) negative statements that you are saying to yourself, then it is worthwhile to seek outside help—whether a therapist, rabbi, priest, or other professional—to help you identify them. After all, you cannot eradicate harmful words that you don't even know are painting an inaccurate picture.

Sometimes I see people who recognize they are repeating the self-hating words that undermine their faith in themselves—they just don't know how to stop doing it. In these cases, I tell people to imagine that these voices are coming from another person, instead of from within them. I actually encourage people to give them aliases, like Bill, Jon, or Debbie. Then when you hear yourself say, "I should never be trusted," you can replace it with "Bill/Jon/Debbie is telling me I am not trustworthy." Taking those voices outside yourself will help you to separate those messages from what you know to be true about yourself. At first this can seem uncomfortable and forced, and it may even give you the giggles. But stay the course, as the end result—being able to distinguish negative voices from what is real—is essential for establishing or reestablishing our faith in ourselves.

Sadly, I often see a pattern in which people *say* that they want to rephrase the negative messaging in their heads but in actuality are not ready. Rather than focusing on how to replace those messages, they focus on how those messages got there. And they get stuck blaming the people and the situations that initiated them.

When I tried to counsel Zoe to recognize the words and thus the ideas about herself that were undermining her faith, she did not want to hear it. She wanted to talk to me about how her parents never, ever allowed her to make a decision. They told her what clothes to buy, whom to date, where to go to college, where to work, and she obediently listened to them. She did not always agree with them, but when she voiced her opinions, they shot her down. They told her, "We know you better." After years of hearing this, she had, understandably, developed the belief that she did not possess decision-making capabilities and she was untrustworthy. She could see the pattern was hurting her, but she did not want to stop blaming them. Staying angry was a great distraction. It allowed her to avoid really looking inside herself.

But staying angry, blaming, and holding on to resentments thwarts our ability to cross thresholds, to move ahead. Eleanor Roosevelt said, "No one can make you feel inferior without your consent." The more time and energy we devote to the people and the words that hurt us, the more authority we give them. By continuing to blame her parents, Zoe was unwittingly consenting to remain "their little girl." She was the helpless victim. They were the nasty perpetrators. Unconsciously she still was handing them the power to dictate how she lived. They might have started the negative patterns, but she was promulgating them.

When I brought this to her attention, she was confused because she really believed that blaming them would eventually heal her. Except we all know that staying angry with the people who may have hurt us ultimately either turns us into someone we don't want to be or prevents us from breaking the mold of someone we once were. Zoe could remain angry with them for a lifetime, or she could begin to let go of her anger and begin to address all the doubts she had about herself.

Sherre Hirsch

Some Difficulties Are Actually Desirable

Our natural tendency is to run away from or ignore things in life that are hard, painful, or challenging, but ignoring those harmful voices won't make them go away. Instead we must face them. Luckily, it turns out that when challenges are put in front of us, they actually force us to think and act in different ways. Every time we do, our brains open up new retrieval pathways. This means that with each challenge, each hardship, each difficulty, we get more practice, more skill, and more opportunities to build our faith.

Mike, for example, had been a successful entrepreneur in a business with his best friend. But in the last few years, though the company had plenty of business, somehow it was not making money. Mike's assistant had urged him to hire an outside accountant to review the books, but he had refused because he "trusted" his best friend. One day he picked up a call not intended for him and overheard his partner arranging to leave their company and start a new one with one of his competitors. Now growing suspicious, he hired the accountant to review the books. Quickly he learned not only that his best friend was planning to leave him in the lurch but also that he had been stealing money for the last four years.

Mike was devastated by the betrayal. He was humiliated and ashamed and, as often happens in these kinds of situations, he began to doubt himself and all the decisions he had made up to this point. How had he been so blind? He berated and doubted himself. He began to question not only his financial decisions of the past but many other decisions as well. Was he in the right profession? Had he married the right person? Now he was broke financially, emotionally, and spiritually as well. He had completely lost faith in himself.

What I said to Mike was that, yes, this experience was devastating, but he could not let it define him in the way he was doing. This experience was not proving that he was blind in business and a bad decision maker. This experience was teaching him a valuable lesson, letting him know that even friends who we think would never do so can betray us. It was teaching him that in the next business venture he would need to be more cautious about whom he partnered with and about his oversight of the partnership.

In that moment Mike thought this experience was the worst thing that had ever happened to him and that he would never recover. Yet a few years later, Mike told me that the betrayal by his partner and the collapse of his business had turned out to be one of the best things that ever happened to him. Of course I was shocked. The best? Really? He explained that since it had put him back at square one, it gave him the opportunity to pursue a new business that had always been his dream. His enthusiasm had become so contagious that his wife, with whom he had always wanted to work but who had never been willing, joined him voluntarily. Now not only was his marriage stronger than ever and his business thriving, but he was loving his work and feeling more faith in himself than ever.

How often do we hear this same story with different

details? A person hits rock bottom, loses their faith, and believes they will never recover. Yet in time they not only survive but thrive—not in spite of the setback but because of the knowledge and personal growth they drew from it.

This is just as true in our personal lives as in our professional ones. When Kim met Joseph, for example, it was true love. They dated for two years and wanted to get married, but he was adamant that she convert to Judaism. Even though she came from a strong Catholic background, she loved him, so she agreed. She spent a year studying and embraced her new tradition, and they soon got engaged. Then, a month before the wedding—the invitations had even been sent—he called it off. She was humiliated and devastated. It was "the worst time of her life." Everyone assumed she would abandon Judaism, but instead she looked to the faith for comfort and solace. She joined a synagogue and started to participate in a singles group. Her family was suspicious, but being a Jew just felt right to her. Eventually she met and fell in love with another Jewish man, who turned out to be the man of her dreams.

In my work I hear stories like this all the time. "I was devastated when I got fired, but it led me to a job I never would have considered." Or "I was heartbroken when my wife left me, but it forced me to look at what kind of husband I was and wanted to be." Most people tell me that even though the pain was real and in the moment they thought they had lost all hope and faith forever, once they were able to reframe it as a growth experience they discovered their faith had been there all along.

Of course, not every situation works out so beautifully as Mike's and Kim's did. Sometimes difficult experiences are just difficult, without an apparent or obvious silver lining. The very worst part of being a rabbi is helping a parent bury their child. I have never told a parent, nor will I ever tell a parent, that this experience has an upside. In this situation I can understand that the parent really believes she will never recover. She really means it when she says she can't imagine ever feeling happy again. In this situation I understand when people lose their faith altogether. But while I would never wish this experience on my worst enemy, I do find, when I encounter these parents years later, that for some it has strengthened them—built their resilience. And in most cases they do eventually find happiness again.

The character of Ruth is revered in the Bible as one of the most iconic models of faith for the Jewish people, even though she lived much of her life as a non-Jew and she endured lots of sadness in her lifetime. The story begins with her future mother-in-law, Naomi, living in Bethlehem, happily married to Elimelech with two sons, Mahlon and Chilion. Then there is a famine and the family is forced to move to Moab. Sadly, Elimelech does not survive. Naomi, now alone, raises Mahlon and Chilion as a single parent. Eventually they meet and marry Moabite (non-Jewish) women, Ruth and Orpah. For the next ten years, the five of them live happily together, until tragedy strikes again and Mahlon and Chilion die. Now Naomi is living in a foreign place with no family besides her two Moabite daughters-in-law, so she decides to move back to Bethlehem.

Since the girls are not her blood, she urges them not to follow her: "Turn back, each of you to your mother's house. There you will find security and a new husband," she tells them. Orpah, heeding her advice, leaves reluctantly to start a new life. But Ruth clings to her mother-in-law. In a heart-wrenching scene, Naomi begs Ruth to follow Orpah but Ruth refuses. She says, "Do not urge me to leave you, to turn back and not follow you. For wherever you go, I will go; wherever you lodge, I will lodge; your people shall be my people and your God, my God. Where you die, I will die and there I will be buried."

What is Ruth thinking? Naomi has no more sons she can marry. The likelihood that she will find another husband in Bethlehem is slim; she will be a widowed, non-Jewish woman living in ancient Israel with her ex-mother-in-law. (Remember, a husband and children defined a woman in ancient Israel.) Naomi has not made her any promises. Naomi has no obligation to her. Ruth could be rejected by the Bethlehem community or even expelled. She could go back to Bethlehem and be alone forever.

So why would Ruth want to go with Naomi? It makes no logical sense, not even to Naomi. But Ruth sees all her past experiences, the love and the heartache, as leading her to this moment, in which she will go with Naomi and live as a Jew. Rather than seeing her hardship as evidence of poor life decisions, she sees it as an opportunity: an opportunity to cross a new threshold in front of her. And so she crosses it to her destiny, her life with Naomi.

Ruth's is one of the most powerful stories of faith that exists in the entire biblical tradition. And it is not a story about faith in God. It is a seminal story about having faith in oneself. And the reason we read it every year on Shavuot, one of the most important Jewish holidays, is to remind us that believing in ourselves is possibly even more important than believing in God.

The Bible is telling us that this is the kind of faith we all need to acquire—the deep-rooted belief that all our past experiences had a purpose in leading us to this moment, that while some of them may have been painful and others confusing, they have all been practice to help us realize important truths about who we are. It's telling us that our choices of the past have not been mistakes. We are not a mistake. We should not run back where we came from. Instead, with faith in our hearts, we should continue onward, crossing new thresholds and trusting in ourselves that the one precious life we construct for ourselves will be a meaningful and rewarding one.

Chapter 3

From the Head to the Heart

I think that if you live long enough, you realize that so much of what happens in life is out of your control, but how you respond to it is in your control. That's what I try to remember.

—Hillary Clinton

A few years ago, while attending a conference in Miami, I heard Jennifer Thompson-Cannino, an adorable, tiny blonde with tremendous passion and eloquence, recount a harrowing story. In 1984, when she was a student at Elon College in North Carolina, a man broke into her house in the night and raped her. As he violated her, she memorized his face, his voice, and everything else about him so that when she survived, as she fully intended to, she would put him in prison for what he did. After the assault was over, she was able to distract him by offering him a drink and fled to a neighbor's house, where she called the police.

A short while later, the police had a few suspects and

she was asked to identify her rapist. With 100 percent confidence she picked Ronald Cotton out of a number of photos. Quickly he was arrested and, despite his repeated claims of innocence, found guilty and sentenced to life in prison.

So you can imagine my surprise—and the surprise of the three hundred other people attending Thompson-Cannino's talk—when a very tall, awkward African American man walked out onto the stage and introduced himself as Ronald Cotton. He spoke softly, continuing the story where Jennifer had left off. When he arrived at prison, he met a man named Bobby Poole, who looked strikingly like him. They became friendly and quickly he learned that Poole had in fact been Jennifer Thompson's rapist—but he had no way to prove it. Who would believe him?

Three years later, there was enough evidence for a retrial, but once again Jennifer Thompson identified Cotton as her rapist, and he was found guilty again. For eleven years he maintained his innocence while Jennifer slept comfortably *knowing* her convicted rapist was in prison for life.

But in 1995, thanks to the discovery of DNA testing, he caught a break. Experts hired by his attorneys were able to recover a tiny sample of sperm from the rape kit from eleven years earlier that proved what he had known all along: he was innocent. He was freed. He began a new life. He found a job, married, had a child, and tried to put the past behind him.

Two years later he received a letter from Jennifer. She wanted to apologize. She was so full of shame and guilt that she could not bear to live with herself. She had no idea how he would react. Would he forgive her? Would he want revenge? She didn't even know if he would read her letter. She was terrified, she recounted to the roomful of people, who were now listening with rapt attention.

Then Cotton spoke again. While he was in prison, he explained, he didn't have control over anything. He was not allowed to choose when to eat, when to sleep. He was told what to do, when to do it, and how to do it. He had lost all his freedoms. But when Jennifer approached him and asked for his forgiveness, he realized he finally had control over *something:* he had control over how to respond.

How could a man who had been so wronged and endured so much suffering as a result still choose to forgive? Think how many times you have had trouble forgiving someone for far less an offense. Your sister for not coming to your son's first birthday party. Your coworker for taking the credit for an idea you came up with. Your husband for flirting with your pretty neighbor. What made it possible for him to forgive in such an extreme situation while so many of us in far less dire circumstances cannot?

When I heard this story, it got me wondering about why it is that people respond so differently from one another during the liminal moments of their lives. Why is it that some jump into action and others get paralyzed? Why is it that some turn inward and others outward? Why do some blame others, some blame themselves, and others never blame at all?

To what degree are we actually in control of our responses during difficult times in our lives? Does our disposition or our genetics play any role in determining how we react?

How Much Control Do We Really Have?

In 1996 University of Minnesota researchers David Lykken and Auke Tellegen studied the role of genes in determining one's sense of satisfaction in life. After they compared the data on four thousand identical and fraternal twins born in Minnesota from 1936 to 1955, they concluded that our genes determine about 50 percent of our happiness in life.* This means that while half of our feelings and responses may be hardwired, a full 40 percent of our happiness—as Martin Seligman at the University of Pennsylvania, who furthered the research, later confirmed—is determined by the conscious choices we make, like the people we choose to engage with, the pleasures we choose to indulge in, and the meaning we choose to discover (the remaining 10 percent is related to circumstantial factors like income, marital status, religion, and education). Now, at first blush, 40 percent may not sound like much, but in reality it is a huge amount. To put this in perspective, think of how excited you would be to get

* David Lykken and Auke Tellegen, "Happiness Is a Stochastic Phenomenon," *Psychological Science* 7 (1996).

a 40 percent raise at work or have a 40 percent larger house or run a marathon 40 percent faster. So imagine what our life would be like if we could make the deliberate choices that would allow us to be a full 40 percent happier.

While modern psychology only recently began studying this finding, the Bible seemed to know it early on. In one famous story Joseph is one of Jacob's twelve sons, but he is clearly his father's favorite. When his father gives Joseph an extraordinary coat, he brags incessantly to his brothers and they become so jealous and resentful of him that they throw him in a pit to die. But at the last minute Judah, one of his brothers, decides to spare Joseph and sells him to a caravan of Ishmaelites, who then sell him to Potiphar, Pharaoh's right-hand man. Joseph works hard. But alas, Potiphar's wife tries to seduce him, and Potiphar, siding with his wife, throws Joseph into prison.

In prison Joseph discovers his gift as a dream interpreter and soon becomes well known for his incredible talent. So when Pharaoh starts having nightmares that he cannot understand, he summons Joseph to his bedside. Joseph accurately interprets Pharaoh's dreams as premonitions of the famine to come, and Pharaoh immediately appoints Joseph to spearhead the effort to prepare Egypt for the famine. Joseph does, and thanks to him, the people of Egypt store enough food over the next seven years so that when the famine comes, they are saved.

Yet Joseph's brothers and father have not prepared for

the famine, as the Egyptians had been advised. So in desperation they go to Pharaoh to ask for provisions in order to survive. As Joseph is the man in charge, they are forced to make an appeal directly to him, but since it has been years, they do not recognize him. He has matured into a man, and he speaks and dresses like an Egyptian. There is no way for them to connect the Joseph of their childhood to the man in front of them.

But Joseph, of course, knows exactly who they are. And in that moment he has to make a decision not unlike the one Ronald Cotton had to make when he received his accuser's apologetic letter: Should I forgive them, or should I exact revenge?

At first Joseph "acted like a stranger to them and spoke harshly to them."* He cannot forgive them, and he wants them to suffer as he did. He questions their motives and claims they are spies. So he decides to test them to see if they have changed their ways. First he demands that one brother go and bring back Benjamin, their youngest brother, while the others stay in prison in Egypt. He then detains them for three days. On the third day, Joseph tells them he intends to keep one of the brothers prisoner while the rest go home and feed their households. As Joseph hears them discuss their distress, he steps away and weeps. Joseph is deeply saddened by the contrition he now knows his brothers feel, but it is not

---

* All quotes in this section are from Genesis 42:7.

enough for him at that moment to forgive them and disclose his identity to them.

When Joseph returns to his brothers, he takes Simeon from them and binds him right before their eyes, telling them that when they return with their youngest brother then he will know that they are not spies. He then orders his stewards to fill his brothers' sacks with the money that they gave to him to pay for their rations, and sends the brothers home to bring back Benjamin.

On their journey home, the brothers discover the money and feel crestfallen because they think that God is framing them. It looks like they have stolen their money back from Joseph so they fear they will be punished. When the brothers get home, they recount some of the events to their father and explain why Benjamin needs to come with them on a second trip back to Egypt.

When they return to Joseph with Benjamin, he frees Simeon as promised. He also gives them water and feeds their animals. Then he inquires of his father, Jacob. Overcome with feeling, he goes into a room and weeps again. Yet he still does not reveal his identity to them.

Still unsure of whether to forgive them, he decides to test them again. This time, as they sit together to dine, Joseph makes sure that Benjamin's portion is several times bigger than that of the other brothers. He wants to see if his obvious favoritism causes the brothers the same jealousy. Will they act in the same way as they had in the past?

He then instructs his stewards to fill the brothers' sacks with food, but to put his own silver goblet in Benjamin's sack. The next day, after the brothers have left the city for home, Joseph sends his stewards after them to find out if they had stolen his goblet. Of course, they hadn't . . . or so the brothers thought. The stewards order them each to open their bag, and there in Benjamin's sack is the silver goblet. The brothers are brought back to the city, and when they arrive, Judah begs Joseph for his forgiveness. He knows that he can't return to his father without Benjamin, so he pleads with Joseph to take him rather than Benjamin.

Joseph's plan to enact revenge had worked. But while it is sweet for a moment, it is clear that it will not bring him happiness. It will not reconcile him with his father. It will not unite them as a family.

It is then that Joseph understands that he cannot go back in time and control or change what has happened to him, but that he can control how he responds in the here and now. In an emotional scene, Joseph "could no longer control himself." He asks his guards to leave him alone with his brothers and then he reveals himself to them. He tells them everything and ensures them he will protect them from the five more years of famine. The brothers are dumbfounded that Joseph is their brother, and Joseph embraces and kisses each brother and weeps. As it is recounted in the Bible, "his sobs were so loud that Egyptians could hear."

The real power of the story of Joseph lies in the fact that he is able to recognize that his initial response is not the right one. And rather than continue to dig his heels in deeper, he is able to step back, evaluate, and ultimately change that response. In other words, one powerful moral of the story is that while we cannot change the past, in changing how we *react* to the past, we can change our future.

To what extent are you like Joseph? When you are wronged, do you want revenge or resolution? When faced with a difficult decision, do you react immediately without thinking, or do you step back and evaluate other possible responses? And when the outcome of your decision doesn't turn out as anticipated, do you stubbornly hold firm or do you reassess and perhaps change course?

In my time as a rabbi I have found that when faced with a difficult choice, most of us tend to react immediately and viscerally, just like Joseph. We are afraid. We are emotional. This is particularly true at liminal moments, when we are feeling even *more* vulnerable and less sure of our decisions and ourselves than normal. Those negative messages we read about in the last chapter drown out any voices of reason, and as a result, our animal brains take over. Luckily, the choice of whether or not to *act* on those fearful voices is entirely up to us.

Feelings Are Not Forever

In times of transition, good or bad, our feelings can be so raw and visceral that we cannot imagine ever feeling any differently than we do at that very moment. When our parent dies, we can feel so abandoned and alone that we can never imagine feeling any other feeling except loss. When we first fall madly in love, we cannot imagine feeling anything but euphoria. When we feel betrayed by a spouse, we can't imagine ever not feeling victimized. We are sure that is how we will feel forever.

But we are bigger than our feelings in any one moment. *Nothing* is forever, especially feelings. Feelings not only change but can change in the blink of an eye. In the movie *500 Days of Summer,* the title character puts it well when she says, "People change. Feelings change. It doesn't mean that the love once shared wasn't true or real." The point is that while your feelings in the moment are real, they are not permanent. Sometimes they disappear altogether. Sometimes they evolve. *How* they change doesn't matter. What matters is that when faced with a difficult decision, you must not let yourself be swayed by your knee-jerk emotions. Instead you must pause. Assess. Evaluate, as Joseph did, whether your choice will make you feel good for one fleeting moment—or whether it will bring you greater happiness over the long haul.

When Leah went into labor at thirty weeks, she was terrified. When her baby was born a few hours later, he was impaired emotionally and physically. He would never talk or walk. He would never become the child she and her husband, Tom, had imagined. They both felt cheated, angry, and very scared. Within a day they decided that they would give the child up for adoption. They knew it was a drastic decision and people would judge them, but they were convinced that they would not be the best parents for such a needy child.

Their doctor, family, and friends tried to convince them that they might eventually feel differently than they did in the moment and that they should wait. But they felt if they waited, then he would never be adopted and it would be too late. They were not callous people; they were realists. They both worked full time and they traveled a lot. How would this child fit into their lives?

So they stuck to their plan and soon a family adopted him. They thought that was the end of their "nightmare." In the next few years they had two healthy children, a boy and a girl, but Leah could not stop thinking about her firstborn. She became more and more depressed, and yet she did not speak of her grief—it was too painful. Of course her husband began to worry about her, but he could not figure out the source of her sadness. One day he came home to find her sobbing in bed. She confided that she desperately missed her son and regretted her decision to give him up for adoption. Tom was shocked because he had thought they were on the same page. And they had been, in those first few days, but with time and perspective the decision that she had been sure was right now felt all wrong.

When they came to me and shared their story, I was devastated for all of them: Leah, Tom, their son, his siblings, both families. There was no good answer. The baby no longer belonged to them, as they had surrendered all their parental rights. Plus, Leah and Tom had begun to argue about it a lot, and now their relationship was in jeopardy. I was not sure what would happen to them.

They went into therapy as I suggested, and they did all the paperwork to request that the adoptive parents reach out to them if they so desired. What I found so amazing is that when the adoptive parents received their request, they immediately contacted Leah and Tom. They said that they wanted their son to meet his biological parents and have a relationship with them. They did not feel threatened. They just wanted him to have all the love possible. It was their kindness that enabled Leah and Tom to form a relationship with their firstborn and move forward both as individuals and as a couple.

One day Leah came in to see me and showed me pictures of all her children. I could see that she had found peace. But it had been at quite a price. She now realized that pain was not forever and that although she had been so sure she would feel a certain way forever, she now knew how untrue that was. Whether our pain stems from something as dramatic as giving up a disabled child or as mundane and ordinary as a setback at work or a fight with a significant other, only by reminding ourselves that our feelings are not forever can we find the strength and courage to move past them.

Sometimes women come to me because their husbands have cheated on them and they are looking for spiritual guidance. Often they are surprised by the very simple advice I give them. *Wait,* I tell them, *before you do anything. Of course, your immediate response will be to yell and scream, throw his clothes out a window, and change the locks. You will want to vilify him to your friends, punish him, and get revenge. That is what you may want to do* today. *But that may not be what you want to do a week or three months or a year from now. And if you wait instead of reacting, other things may happen during those windows. He may beg for your forgiveness; you may forgive him; or you may find you want to reconcile with him whether he has changed or not. Or you may meet someone else, fall in love, and move on.*

This is not to give him a free pass, I tell these women; *it is to give* you *one. Because the fact is, you can't change the past, and reacting out of your negative and hurt emotions will not do anything for your future—except possibly make you even more resentful.* I have yet to meet the person whose life goal is to be angry and bitter. And while it's natural to feel those emotions in the moment, acting on them will only lead to more hurt and more regret as time marches on.

The Wait Box

I'll be the first to admit that when it comes to emotion, restraint is not always my strong suit. When I was a pulpit rabbi, I frequently got calls from congregants who felt that someone in their lives had treated them unfairly. My initial reaction was always very visceral; as a rabbi I felt I needed to right the wrong. And often I spoke out of turn. I thought I knew the entire story, but all I really knew was that person's perspective on the injustice of their situation. But usually, over time, I would see that there was a bigger picture and that my emotional response hadn't achieved anything beyond giving that congregant license to feel even more hurt and indignant and angry. And I in turn would feel regret and remorse.

To combat this tendency I developed the Wait Box, a file on my computer that still exists today. Whenever I am tempted to react viscerally to a person or a situation, I write my response—holding nothing back—and file it in the Wait Box. There my emotional response sits for twenty-four hours and marinates. Of course, rarely does the response I initially write ever see the light of day. Usually it gets dumped in the trash and later replaced with something much more thoughtful, logical, and productive.

What if each one of us developed a Wait Box for life? What if anytime we were tempted to react immediately—particularly at a critical threshold or liminal moment—we instead jotted those thoughts down . . . and then waited? What if instead of reacting to a lost promotion by storming into our boss's office and quitting our job (like Tom Cruise in the movie *Jerry Maguire*), or instead of responding to a disagreement with our significant other by insisting on breaking up, or instead of letting a potentially life-changing decision be guided by fear, rage, anger, or even love, we forced ourselves to wait just twenty-four hours before responding? Imagine how differently you would relate to people in your life. Imagine how differently other people would relate to you.

You might think, *Of course waiting makes sense when your response is negative, but what about when your gut response is a positive one? Should you still wait?* Yes. Many times our gut response is positive, but that doesn't make it right. Positive or negative, it takes distance and time to determine definitively whether our initial instincts are productive or not. There is *always* value in waiting and letting the thoughtful response catch up with the emotional one.

Plus, when we wait and respond calmly instead of out of raw emotion, our message has a better chance of getting through. When someone is heated and angry, it is hard to hear him or her. This is why parents are counseled again and again to whisper rather than yell when they are angry with their children, as it is a more effective way of getting the children to hear their frustration. It is a truism that all people are more receptive when they are spoken to from a thoughtful and restrained place. When we wait, we have a better chance of being able to communicate more effectively *and* be heard more clearly.

Often the quicker we are to react to something, the longer-lasting the consequences. Fred and Elise were newly married. Fred was used to being the single guy and going out every night. A short time into their marriage he started to feel "tied down." But rather than talking to her about the fact that he had started to suffocate, he would just go out with his buddies without telling her. She would worry and call his cell phone but he would ignore it. After trying many times to speak to him about it, one day Elise had finally had enough and told him she was leaving. It was only then that Fred realized that he had been acting solely out of fear and resentment and that he had almost lost his marriage—forever—as a result. It took her threatening to leave him for him to realize that he needed to change the way he responded to her. And he did.

Sometimes our emotions can be so blinding that it takes someone else to point out the long-lasting consequence of our responses. Angela and her husband, for example, were married for sixteen years with three children when they went through a horrible divorce. They fought incessantly and spent thousands of dollars on legal fees. It got to the point that Angela could barely stand to look at him; when he came to pick up the children from her house, the children waited outside on the curb while she watched from the window. And when it was her turn to pick up the children from his house, she sent the nanny.

This went on for years. And each day the children watched their parents' hatred grow. Then one day, her daughter told Angela that she would never marry because if it did not work out, the hatred would kill her. At that moment Angela realized that while she couldn't change what had happened between her and her husband in the past, she could change the way she responded to him in the present and future. She realized that little by little, with each hateful glance, with each venomous comment, she was killing not only her own soul but her children's as well. Her hatred had become a disease that was infecting their family. Instead of modeling for her impressionable children the power of love, she was showing them the power of hate.

Once her daughter forced her to see the long-term consequences of her emotional reactions, she reached out to her ex-husband. At first he was reluctant to even speak to her. What did she want from him now? But eventually he realized that he too had been responding to her solely out of anger and saw how much it was hurting the people they loved.

They did not get back together. They did not become best friends. This is not a Lifetime TV movie. But they did find a way to improve how they interacted. They made a conscious decision to change how they spoke to each other—and how they spoke about each other. They even changed the carpool arrangements so that their children could wait in the house when the other parent picked them up. Had their children never said anything, they might have continued down the vicious spiral of hate forever, but thankfully they did not.

When you see a loved one responding in ways that are sabotaging their happiness, it can be hard to know whether it's your place to speak up. At what point are you simply helping them recognize that holding on to all their negative emotions is detrimental? And at what point are you being critical and intrusive?

I saw this dilemma most clearly when my brother's best friend since childhood died of Hodgkin's disease a few months after his senior year in college. We were all devastated, but his mother in particular was demolished, understandably. As the months wore on, however, instead of moving forward with her life and living with his loss, she seemed to only be getting worse. She quit her job; she stopped socializing. The more time passed, the more the grief paralyzed her.

We all loved his mother so much, but we were not sure at what point we should talk to her about her behavior. Finally, after about two years, one of her dear friends—another parent who had been with her from the diagnosis onward and who had cared, empathized, and related to her for years—spoke honestly, sharing all of our collective concerns for her. At first she was taken aback, but over time she started to reenter her life. She returned to work. She started to reconnect with her friends. She even started talking about creating a foundation in her son's memory. She finally understood that while she would never get over her grief, she could find a way to use it to bring new meaning and purpose to her life. And while I would like to believe that eventually she could have come to that realization on her own, I do believe that it was the caring friend's courage to reach out and help her change her response that made the difference. It is now twenty years later and her foundation has impacted over a million children with cancer around the world.

It Is Up to You

Often it is tempting to believe that how we act in liminal moments is dictated by the situation itself. If the situation involves betrayal, we feel we are entitled to be angry. If the situation involves loss, we feel we are entitled to be devastated. Wouldn't we all like to justify our responses by the external circumstances?

But at the same time, isn't it a relief to know that we are *not* powerless in the face of external forces? To the contrary. How we choose to respond is not based on the incident; it is based on us.

How many times have you witnessed one person get fired from a job and see it as the end of their career while another person sees it as an opportunity to begin a new chapter? Or seen one person be utterly devastated by the death of a loved one while another person chooses to focus on all the amazing things the loved one achieved in his or her life? The point is that every day we see people respond to the liminal moments of their lives so differently; if our responses were controlled by external forces, how could this be possible?

As a rabbi I have spent a lot of time with people who are facing illnesses. Sometimes I will find myself counseling two people being treated for the exact same disease. It never ceases to amaze me that even when their dispositions and external circumstances are as similar as can be, how they respond to their situation differs vastly.

When my mother was being treated for stage-two breast cancer, the same physician was treating another woman for the exact same diagnosis. They were about the same age, came from similar backgrounds, and even had similar personalities; they were so alike that the doctor became certain the two of them would become friends—so certain that he actually scheduled them to receive treatment at the same time. When my mother first heard this, she was thrilled to have a person to talk to who was sharing her experience, someone who would understand like no one else. My mother imagined finding a friend for life.

Except this was not what happened at all. When they first met, it was true that outwardly they had a lot in common. But they did not connect as the physician and my mother had thought they would.

The difference? The beliefs they held about their illness. My mother would exercise and try to eat right. The other woman thought those lifestyle changes were pointless. My mother would socialize with other patients in the chemo ward; the other woman would quietly hide in the corner. My mom believed it would soon all be behind her, as the doctor assured her, while the other woman doubted him immensely and thought she would always be sick. They had the exact same prognosis, but how they chose to respond to it could not have been more different.

As a result, the two of them had very little to talk about, and I could see it was frustrating for both of them.

Each one wanted the other to respond the way she did. My mother wanted someone to echo her optimism; the other woman wanted my mother to share in her suffering. What made it even worse was that each would try to convince the other to change her response. My mother would bring the other woman articles on eating right, and the other woman would bring articles on the importance of writing your will. (Spoiler alert: They both made full recoveries. My mother did not die from breast cancer; she died about five years later from an entirely unrelated brain cancer.)

On the way home from her treatments, my mother would tell me just how frustrated she was. She was sure that this woman's negative attitude not only was wrong but would hamper her recovery. My mother wanted desperately for me to join her in her condemnation of this woman. I was tempted, but instead I would remind my mother (and myself) that how we act in liminal moments—particularly the difficult ones—is a choice that each one of us gets to make for ourselves. No one else gets to make it for us.

By the same token, we cannot dictate the response of another human being no matter how much we might want to. We can point out how their response is hurting them, as the friend of the grief-stricken parents did in the story above, but we cannot change it. Nor should we judge. This is why I counsel families again and again that when a person they love is standing at a threshold—whether it is a wedding or a funeral or something in between—to withhold judgment about how that person is responding. You may be tempted to try to change their behavior. But you have to resist—no matter how much you might disagree or feel hurt by it. If your mother is sick and your sibling does not come to the hospital as much as you do, let it be. If your father dies and your mother starts dating right away, don't judge. If you are getting married and your best friend is not as enthusiastic as you had hoped she would be, hold your tongue. There are other times and places in our lives when it's appropriate to be a little judgmental, but liminal moments like these—ones that are so fraught with all kinds of emotions—are not among them.

The Mussar movement, an ethical wing of Judaism that developed in the nineteenth century, teaches us to pause before we judge another and ask ourselves, *What is their fear?* The point of this question is to force you to interrupt your judgment and instead recognize that most of the time people are afraid, and their responses are driven by their fears. The Mussarians believe that just in asking this question we can transform our judgment into compassion and even love.

In the liminal moments of our lives, when we are thrust into a situation or transition that shocks, confuses, or stumps us, it can often be difficult to see that while we may not have control over the situation, we do have control over how we respond. It is easy, in the throes of the uncertainty and anxiety that accompany these moments, to be blind to all the different courses of action. It is a long way from the head to the heart.

Yet moving forward across the threshold requires that we summon the faith and the courage to act from the head and not the heart. It requires that instead of succumbing to the heat of our emotions we step back, pause, and take stock. It requires that we remind ourselves that, while our feelings in the moment are very real, they are not permanent. And that if we react out of our visceral, gut responses, we may end up doing long-term damage—to others, to our relationships, to ourselves—that cannot be undone. Above all, it requires that if we remember nothing else we remember this: while we will never be fully in control of our external circumstances, how we choose to act in those circumstances is entirely up to us.

Chapter 4

Perfection Is Not a Destination

When you aim for perfection, you discover it's a moving target.

—Geoffrey F. Fisher

On January 22, 1990, Random House published *Oh, the Places You'll Go!*, by Theodor Seuss Geisel, aka Dr. Seuss. It became one of the best-selling of the forty-six books he wrote in his lifetime and remains *the* graduation gift for every high school and college senior. Even though Dr. Seuss never spoke publicly about his personal connection to the book, he could have written this story only with the perspective and hindsight of having lived a life in which he had to cross many thresholds.

Though he ultimately attained hundreds of accolades and tremendous professional success, Dr. Seuss had a life filled with ups and downs. His first book was rejected twenty-seven times by publishers, and he struggled financially in the early years of his career. He married his love, Helen, but later in life she committed suicide. And of course these are the details that are public; I am sure he experienced countless other challenges that we will never be privy to.

In *Oh, the Places You'll Go!* Dr. Seuss was essentially talking about thresholds. If you continue crossing them, his story is saying, you will go to rooms in which things will happen. Some will lead you where you dreamed you could be: "You'll join the high fliers who soar to high heights." But some will take you to a place that is tougher and rougher than you thought possible: "You can get all hung up in a prickle-ly perch. And your gang will fly on. You'll be left in a Lurch." Others will confuse you: "You will come to a place where the streets are not marked. Some windows are lighted. But mostly they're darked." And some will lead you to fear: "There are some, down the road between hither and yon, that can scare you so much you won't want to go on."

But in the end Dr. Seuss asks and answers, "And will you succeed? Yes! You will, indeed! (98 and ¾ percent guaranteed.)"

Dr. Seuss wanted us to realize that crossing thresholds is not like climbing a ladder. Each rung does not necessarily directly lift us closer to our goal. The hallways of our lives are more like a labyrinth. They can be very circuitous and unexpected. Often we may not even know which direction we're going, yet keep going we must, because the route will eventually lead us to the room that is 98 and ¾ percent right for us.

This is what happens to Yocheved, the mother of Moses, in the famous Bible story. When she and her husband, Amram, become pregnant with their first child, Pharaoh has decreed that all the firstborn male children be put to death. So when Moses is born, it seems their son's fate is sealed. He will be killed. But in a desperate attempt to save her child, Yocheved hides her baby for three months—despite the risk that she and her husband will be discovered and put to death. Eventually, however, his cries get so loud that she can no longer hide him.

She is not sure what to do. It is not as if she has a lot of choices. So, desperate again, she places him in a small ark and floats him down the Nile River. I imagine in that moment she feels this is the only alternative to certain death at the hands of Pharaoh, despite the very strong possibility that he either will be discovered and killed or will drown in the river. Either way, in Yocheved's mind, his fate is sealed.

But Moses's older sister, Miriam, keeps an eye on her baby brother as he floats away. Pharaoh's daughter discovers the baby in the basket in the river and decides to keep him. Miriam takes this opportunity to ask the princess if she would like her to fetch from the Hebrew women a woman to nurse the baby. Immediately Pharaoh's daughter tells her, "Go" and Miriam promptly fetches Moses's mother to be the wet nurse for her son. Thus Moses is returned to his mother but no longer at risk of being killed, as he is now under the Pharaoh's daughter's protection. As the story goes, once he is old enough, Yocheved brings the boy to Pharaoh's daughter who then adopts him and names him Moses.

Can you imagine Yocheved's dilemma? Does she refuse the opportunity, sparing herself the future pain of having to give him away again? She has already let him go once; can she do it again? Wouldn't it be easier to erase his memory forever and move on with her life?

Or does she agree to the conditions and then defy the decree? Does she nurse him, reveal her identity, and secretly plan to never give him back? Does she run away? None of her options are great or even close to good. They will all cause her—and possibly her husband and her child—pain, suffering, and even danger.

She cannot delay for long, as Pharaoh's daughter is waiting. So with trepidation and anticipation she agrees to nurse him with all the conditions attached. When she holds him in her arms again, it must be bittersweet. He is alive and safe, yes, but she will never be his "mother." And in a short time she will have to give him back.

What I imagine Yocheved realizes is that if she refuses the offer altogether, it is almost certain that she will never see him again, and their story will be permanently over. But if she agrees, there is at least a chance, however small, that something may happen to change her—and his—fate.

Maybe Pharaoh's daughter will change her mind. Maybe in time she will decide that she doesn't want to raise him after all. Maybe Yocheved's identity will be revealed by some happenstance and Pharaoh's daughter will find compassion and give Moses back to her. Maybe something will happen to Pharaoh's daughter that will render her unfit to take him back in three years' time—or ever. Maybe Pharaoh's daughter will come to value Yocheved so much that she will hire her to raise him to adulthood as his nanny. Yocheved must be reasoning that at the very least she will be with her son for a few years—which is longer than she ever thought she'd have with him when she sent him down the river.

Yocheved has no way of knowing where her decision will ultimately lead. But she decides to cross the threshold anyway and see what happens. She knows there are no guarantees that the next room will be better than the last—that taking him and giving him up again in three short years will be any less painful than saying good-bye to him permanently now. But she also knows that if she *doesn't* take him, the door to a better room—a room in which she can raise her son as his real mother—will shut, possibly forever.

We often find ourselves in similar shoes. Maybe the choice we are deliberating isn't as dramatic as the fate of our son, but throughout our lives we'll all face myriad choices for which the outcome is uncertain and the options are far from ideal.

Take Alison, who came to me seeking advice about her elderly mother. At ninety-one Estelle was no longer the spry, independent firecracker that she had always been, and it was becoming abundantly obvious to Alison and her husband that it was no longer safe for her to live by herself in her apartment. They had been trying to talk to her about other living arrangements for several years, and she had refused to listen, but now the situation had become grave and it was critical that Alison and her husband find her mother an alternative living situation. The problem was that none of the options available were right for Estelle—or for Alison.

Estelle wanted a private nurse to care for her day and night in her apartment, but they did not have the means. Thus she was left with only two options: either move to the local nursing home that was covered by her insurance or move three thousand miles away to live with Alison and her family. Neither was an attractive choice; Estelle had been saying her whole life that she would never, ever move to a nursing home, that she would die before her daughter made her. And Estelle had also been adamant that she would never live on the East Coast with her daughter. Not only did she hate the weather and have no friends there, but she didn't want to burden her daughter and her family. Estelle knew that Alison and her husband were already strapped financially, that their marriage was shaky, and that her moving in would make an already rocky situation even rockier.

Alison knew she had to make a tough choice, but as Estelle's health worsened, she became more and more paralyzed by indecision. For a long while she held on to the false hope that something or someone would intervene to resolve the situation for her. Maybe her mother would come around to the nursing home idea, or maybe she would magically come into a windfall of money. Like Yocheved, Alison could not let go of the hope that some divine fate would intervene. So when this didn't happen, and it finally became clear to her she had no choice but to choose between her equally unattractive options, she was even more distraught. Plus, now she was also upset that she had postponed deciding for so long and allowed the situation to devolve into this mess that needed urgent attention but had no immediately obvious solution.

So, like Yocheved, she made the best choice she could. She moved her mother across the country to live with her and her family. It was a huge effort and a lot of expense, but at least she knew that finally her mother would be safe and cared for. But life on the East Coast turned out to be very lonely for Estelle. Alison and her husband worked all day and their teenage children were consumed with their schoolwork and activities, so Estelle spent most of her day watching TV and becoming bitter at her daughter for having put her in this unhappy situation.

Then, eight months later, Alison got an unexpected promotion with a nice boost in pay. Suddenly she and her husband could afford to hire a part-time caretaker for her mother—someone who could keep Estelle company and take her to social outings and activities during the day. This turned out to make all the difference; it allowed Estelle to eventually make a life for herself in her daughter's home in Baltimore, where she lived, fairly contentedly, for another four years until she died at age ninety-six.

But while this story has a relatively happy ending, for

Alison the road there was even bumpier than it appeared. She loved her mother and was happy that she could accommodate her in her home and give her the company she needed. But it was hard having her mother living with them. Alison felt responsible for her and often worried that she was putting her mother's needs ahead of the needs of her children, her husband, and even herself. After all, she and her husband could have used that money she earned from her promotion to help their children with college, plan for their retirement, or even go on a much-needed vacation. And even though she had talked to her husband about how to use those additional funds and was happy to be able to give her mom what she needed in the last years of her life, she also felt guilty and sad that she had to prioritize her mother at the expense of her family at times.

In the end, though, Alison realized that even though their choice had been difficult and the path not exactly smooth, it had certainly turned out better than the alternative. Stepping up and taking action by moving her mother out to Baltimore—rather than letting her live out her days alone in her West Coast apartment—had been the right decision; if she hadn't, and something had happened to her mother as a result of the lack of care and supervision, Alison would never have been able to forgive herself. Plus, although those last years hadn't been a walk in the park, having their grandmother live with them had brought Alison's children closer to not only Estelle but also to each other, which gave all of them a lot of peace when she died. Years later Alison was able to reflect and see that while the situation had not been ideal, it had yielded many unexpected benefits that she could never have anticipated.

What Do We Do When All Our Options Suck?

Often when we are faced with a decision where all the options, frankly, kind of suck, we do what Alison tried doing at first. We wait for a while, hoping that something will happen and rescue us from having to choose between our "not great" options. Sometimes this strategy works. Occasionally another option presents itself and our dilemma is resolved in a way that we never expected. But more often than not, there is no divine intervention. And now, by delaying, we have compounded the problem. Not only do we feel guilty for having postponed our decision, but there may be repercussions of our having waited. Some of the less bad options may no longer be available to us, which can make us even more distressed and frustrated. Now, in addition to the pressure of making a decision, we have all these other negative feelings weighing on us.

So how do we find the strength to cross a threshold when the rooms awaiting us are far from perfect? First we need to let go of the whole notion of a "perfect" outcome.

As someone who has counseled many individuals at this very type of liminal moment, I see the same patterns repeated time and time again. But one in particular always stands out.

When it comes to crossing thresholds, people tend to see their options in a very binary way. They believe there is one "right" decision that will lead to what they deem the perfect room. All the other options are, of course, wrong—wrong because people do not perceive them as leading directly to that one "perfect room." Their vision is so clouded by this black-and-white thinking, they become blinded to the fact that there are many other options, many other rooms that, while perhaps not "perfect," will ultimately lead to a place that is right for them.

This binary thinking is flawed from the outset. There is no "perfect" room, as much as we try to convince ourselves otherwise. Therefore it follows that there can be no perfect choice or perfect option—and when believing otherwise leads to inertia or inaction, when it prevents us from crossing the threshold, that's when we get into trouble.

A classic example of this is the way many parents behave when it comes time to enroll their children in preschool. Where I live in Los Angeles, it is highly competitive to get a child into the "best" preschool. (I understand it is the same way in many other big cities.) But while certain preschools are *perceived* as being so much better than others, in reality most of the preschools in the area are very good (after all, preschoolers pretty much do the same things—they eat, they play, they nap—no matter where they attend preschool, so how much variance can there really be?). Yet somehow there is this universal belief that if your child does not go to the "right" preschool, she will not get into the right elementary, then high school, and of course college. Therefore if you do not make the right decision for your child at age two, or so the thinking goes, her fate is sealed, just as Yocheved believed Moses's was; she essentially could be out on the street by the time she is twenty-one.

Of course I am exaggerating the narrative, but not the point, which is that we have become a society that believes everything falls into two buckets: there are things that are perfect and then everything else, which is far from it. So if our decision to cross a threshold does not lead directly to perfect, our reasoning goes, then why bother?

Well, I have proof that many children in Los Angeles, New York, and other cities who have *not* gone to the "perfect preschool" have still gone to good colleges and on to lead very successful lives. So there seems to be at least some reason to bother.

Perfection Is Not a Destination

When we think of a "perfect" place, it's hard not to think of the Garden of Eden. There Adam and Eve had no needs or wants. They had everything they could possibly dream of. But if things were so perfect, why was Eve even tempted by the serpent when he tried to convince her to defy God's one condition that they not eat from the Tree of Knowledge of

Good and Evil? She wasn't hungry. She wasn't unhappy. But she was curious. And so she indulged and was expelled to the outside world. So while the Garden of Eden may have seemed "perfect" to Adam and Eve in the beginning, well, we all know how long that lasted.

Maybe that is what the Bible is telling us. Stop chasing perfection as if it were a destination, a static place. Stop trying to figure out how to get "there," because when you get there, it will still be lacking, no matter how perfect it appeared from a distance. Perfect, in other words, is a fiction. There is no perfect decision. There is no perfect spouse or house or job or family or anything else—no matter how we might wish it to be otherwise.

Greek philosophers coined the word *eudemonia,* which means "good of all goods, perfection." It is the highest good for human beings. They agreed that *eudemonia* was essentially living well, faring well, and therefore being happy. But as Aristotle pointed out in his writings, "Verbally there is a very general agreement; for both the general run of men and people of superior refinement say that is [eudemonia], and identify living well and faring well with being happy; but with regard to what [eudemonia] is they differ, and the many do not give the same account as the wise."*

In other words, in our quest to find that universal perfect place we often fail to take into account that we are different

---

* Aristotle, *Nicomachean Ethics,* 1095a17.

from one another, and our needs and wants are not the same as everyone else's. There is no universal recipe for happiness, as much as we try to think there is. Harvard may be the best college for one gifted student but not for another. A white picket fence may be idyllic for one family, but for another it might just be plain ugly.

The real danger is when we try to compare our situation in life to other people's, when we look at everyone around us and ask ourselves, *Do they appear to be happy? Fulfilled? Perfect?* (Fill in your own adjective here.) Then we wonder, *Why don't I feel the same way? What is wrong with me?* But comparing ourselves to others is almost certain to lead to feelings of inferiority and dissatisfaction. For example, there is no way to be the perfect mom. Yet all day long, women around the world are trying to be; you know, the mom who works full time at home, volunteers at the school, makes all the lunches, drives her kids to and from all their activities. But this vision of perfection could not be further from reality.

Making matters worse is the fact that each mother believes every other one is the perfect mom. Why? Because mothers rarely talk honestly to one another. When they do greet one another, rather than talking about how their kids can really be a pain in the arse, they pretend that everything is just great. And then each one walks away imagining the other one has mastered motherhood—and that she is the one who is doing it wrong. And so the stay-at-home mom thinks maybe if she were more like the mom who works full time, her kids would be better behaved, while at the same time the mom who works full time outside the home questions her decisions daily and contemplates whether she should change her schedule so her kids can be more like the kids of the full-time mother . . . and so on.

Jill Churchill said, "There's no way to be a perfect mother and a million ways to be a good one."* The same goes for all the other roles we play in our lives. It is not wrong to question the decisions we make along the way and whether they fit us today, but it is wrong to assume that there is one perfect way. No one has a lock on the perfect room, as much as we try to give the impression that we do.

If we want to overcome our (very human) instinct to measure our happiness against the happiness we see around us, first we have to realize that our perception of others' happiness is often very wrong. We see in others only what they want us to see—and often what they want us to see is far from how things actually are. No one posts on Facebook about how imperfect his marriage is. Instead, he posts a picture of himself on his anniversary, celebrating eighteen years of marital bliss. Yet when we see this, it is easy to forget that that picture is just a snapshot of a moment that captures how he wants to present himself to us.

As a rabbi I see this firsthand all the time. I can't even count the number of times I have sat with someone as they described to me another person's life that they wish they had.

---

* Jill Churchill, *Grime and Punishment* (New York: Avon, 1989).

As I listen to them I want to shout out, "Are you kidding me?" We have no idea what goes on in other people's homes. But we do an excellent job of imagining their perfect lives.

Worse still is our tendency to think that we *should* feel the same way as everyone else. If another person seems fulfilled in their job, we think we should be fulfilled in that same job. But we forget that we are entirely different people. Of course we know this intellectually, yet we still spend a lot of time putting pressure on ourselves to be "perfect," as we imagine everyone else to be.

Take the bride planning her wedding. Almost every bride-to-be has the false perception that all the other brides are overflowing with happiness and she is the only one who is stressed and overwhelmed. Similarly, almost every college freshman thinks all his friends are having the time of their lives and he is the only one who secretly thinks college is just okay. (By the way, no matter how many times people say that college was the best years of their lives, it is a lie according to science. Statistically people are the happiest in their sixties, not when they are in college or even as children.) And almost every mourner says to me at some point that other people are handling their grief so much better than he or she is.

I call this syndrome—the belief that everyone else is so much happier than we are—the "just me" disease. We believe we are the only one whose life isn't perfect. And therefore we spend a lot of time chasing the perfection we will never achieve.

Recently I was with a number of families of children

with learning differences. I was sure that since all of these parents had children who were deemed "imperfect" by society that the "just me" disease would not exist. I could not have been more wrong. Parents were quietly comparing their child's deficits with others' and automatically assuming that those children's parents were happier, were dealing with things better, were less in denial.

We need to realize that there is no universally perfect room where we all fit. And we need to stop trying to make decisions that we think will land us in that room that looks like it's so perfect for others. Just because a room might be right for our friend, our coworker, or our neighbor doesn't mean that room is right for us.

We Are Not Psychics

Not only are different rooms more "right" for some individuals than for others, but also different rooms are more right for us at different times in our lives. This is because who we are—and what we want and need—is not static. We are constantly changing emotionally, physically, and spiritually. At one point the perfect job might have been the one that paid a lot. So what if it had long hours? You were single and you did not have a lot of responsibilities outside of your work. But now that you are older, the perfect job might be the one that does not pay as much but gives you a better quality of life, the one that leaves you time to coach your children's Little League on Wednesdays and play golf on Fridays. And at yet another time in your life, the perfect job may be the one that allows you to mentor others. All of these jobs may be "right" for you, but not all at the same time in your life.

This is often confusing and hard to understand because we tend to think that what felt good and right at one time should feel good and right always. And when it doesn't, rather than acknowledging that we have changed—and that we need to change our expectations or situation to bring them in line with *how* we have changed—we instead become frustrated and may begin to blame everyone and everything else around us.

When I met Gwen and Mark they were struggling tremendously. They had dated for five years and been married for five more. They had agreed from the get-go not to have children, and at the time the decision had felt completely right. But as time passed, Mark began to realize that he wanted children after all. However, when he brought it up to Gwen, she was infuriated; that was not the marriage that they had agreed upon. But he was just as furious at her response: he had not had a crystal ball at the time they made that agreement, so why should he be held to it? After all, it was ten years later, and now he felt differently. The arrangement that had once felt right and good to him now felt lacking. They each felt betrayed by the other for changing in ways that they did not expect or plan for.

I get it. We cannot anticipate how we are going to feel in the future. We try to predict because we think we know ourselves. But even though we may know ourselves, we don't always know who we will be five, ten, or twenty years from now. We can know how we feel about the room we are in today, but we don't know how we are going to feel about that room in the future, and we certainly don't know how we are going to feel about a room that we have never experienced before. We can guess how we are going to feel then based on how we feel now. But often we are wrong.

The "planning fallacy" (a term first coined by Daniel Kahneman and Amos Tversky in 1979) proposes that we underestimate how long it will take us to do something because of our inability to predict the future. What Kahneman and Tversky discovered is that only after we have done something many times do we become more accurate in estimating how long it will take—essentially in imagining the future. Our feelings are deeply tied to our imagination. So when we can't imagine the room that we are entering or we can only imagine a piece of it, it is truly hard for us to predict how we will feel when we get there.

Ask a new groom. Ask a new parent. Ask a new retiree. They all say the same thing. They imagined the new room—married life, parenting, retirement—would be a certain way. They had done the research, talked to friends, read the literature. But once they actually crossed the threshold into that room, all the homework in the world had not prepared them.

They thought it was going to be *just perfect* and it turned out to be anything but. It is not that it was horrible (although that happens); it just felt very different from how they thought it would. We all know what it's like to have an idealized vision of the future that in reality does not pan out.

When Elizabeth lost forty-five pounds, for example, she was sure that she was going to feel sexy, beautiful, and happy. She was sure that crossing the threshold from a size sixteen to a size six would fix her life, that she would no longer feel resentment, jealousy, and anger. But when she put on those high-school jeans that had been hanging in her closet forever, her feelings did not melt away as her weight had. She felt healthier and in better shape, true, but all the issues that had led to her weight problem in the first place did not magically disappear. She still had all her fears and insecurities. She still had disappointments and frustrations. Even though the new room was infinitely better than the one from which she had come, it wasn't perfect in the way she had imagined.

So our goal should not be to see into the future and predict what will be the perfect room or the perfect choice. Nor should our goal be to wait for the perfect room or the perfect choice to magically present itself, because more likely than not, we'll be waiting a very long time. Instead, our goal should be to make a decision that reflects what would be best for us in the moment, knowing that it may turn out differently from or totally opposite of how we thought it might. Yes, there is always the chance that we will make a mistake.

Which is why we need to have faith in ourselves to evaluate clearly whether where we have landed is right for us now, or whether we need to cross a different threshold.

How Do We Make the Best Decision Today?

Making a decision that is right for who we are now is really challenging because we don't always know who we are and what we need and what we want in this moment. There are many times in our lives where we lose our sense of self. It happens to the best of us, and not just when we are teenagers trying to find our identity. Maybe something rocked our world: we were fired, or we had a miscarriage, or our spouse left us unexpectedly. Or maybe we got into the habit of letting others shape our identity and make our decisions. Maybe there is no obvious reason; we just feel lost in our lives.

The irony is that these are often the times when it's most critical to cross the threshold. After all, if we're feeling lost in the room we are in, why stay there? Many times I have counseled people that when they feel lost or uncertain, moving forward into a new room—even if it is very imperfect—may be the best way to find answers. Sometimes it is only by making a decision to cross into the wrong room that the threshold to the right one can possibly be revealed. In her best-selling book, *Lean In,* Sheryl Sandberg tells the story of one particular employee, Lori Goler (coincidentally, a friend of mine from young adulthood), who wanted to ascend at Facebook in a new area of expertise but saw no jobs available at her level. Sheryl offered her a lower position, with no guarantees that it would ever lead to where Lori wanted to go, and was surprised and impressed when Lori jumped at it. Lori knew that she ultimately wanted to do what was best for the company, and that sometimes you reach your destination by a different road; other times, a road you choose can lead you to someplace you never expected to go but nevertheless a place that you come to really enjoy (which is exactly what happened to Lori).

Not Even God Is Perfect

I often tell people that I am a B+ mother and I have a B+ marriage, and they always laugh. They think I am joking. I am not. They think, *Who wants to be a B+? Be an A!*

Not me. I strive to be a B+. I strive to be very good, not perfect. Because I know that very good is possible, while perfect is not.

I did not know this from the get-go. It took me a while to learn. For example, in the first few years of my marriage I thought that anytime the tiniest thing was awry in the relationship, we were on our way to divorce. I had this naive belief that any marriage that was less than perfect was doomed.

Had I been paying more attention in Hebrew school

when I was younger, I would have spared myself a lot of anxiety. In the first few chapters of the Bible, we learn that God created the world in six days, and on the seventh day God rested. After the first day, when God separated the light from the darkness, He saw the light as good. On the second day, God made no comment. On the third day, when God created the earth and the seas, He saw what He created as good again. On the fourth day, when God created the stars and the sun and placed them in the sky to shine upon the earth, He saw it as good again. And even on the fifth day, when God created the animals, He saw it as good. But on the sixth day, when God created man, He said, "This is *not* good." Right away, God realized that creating Adam without a companion was a mistake because Adam was so lonely. In an attempt to go from *not good* to at least *better,* He created Eve to be Adam's companion and then He blessed the two of them. Then, in an attempt to summarize all the work of the past few days, "God saw all that He had made and found it very good."*

God did not say that everything was perfect. In adding the "very" to the phrase after a long week of work, God was telling us that we do not need to aim for perfect. God was telling us that it is enough to strive to end each day able to say "good" and some days even to say "very good."

God was not a perfectionist. God did not look for all

* Genesis 1:31.

the mistakes and imperfections in his work. And God was genuinely pleased in what He had created. So why did God ultimately destroy this world with a flood and start all over?

God did not need a 100 percent perfect world, but He did not want a horrific one either. Only when the people started behaving horribly did God begin to question what He had created. It was then that God realized, *Wait, I need to do this again—not with the hope of getting it perfect this time, but with the hope of getting it better than the last time around.*

I don't imagine God beating Himself up or thinking He was a failure for not creating the perfect world on His first attempt. And neither should we beat ourselves up for not immediately choosing the perfect room or reaching the perfect destination.

God teaches us that we must keep moving forward, even when the choices are not great and the outcomes seem far from perfect. Because only when we let go of the myth of perfection can we begin to enjoy and embrace all the very good opportunities, experiences, and adventures that lie ahead.

Chapter 5

Broader Vision, Broader Possibility

It's as if when I open myself up to every perception, things create their own focus.

—Kristin Cashore, *Graceling*

In 1951 the football teams of Dartmouth and Princeton, fierce rivals, played a distinctly brutal game—so brutal that the Princeton quarterback walked off the field in the second quarter with a broken nose and a concussion. By the third quarter the Dartmouth quarterback's leg was broken. At the time it made headlines for being one of the fiercest games in college football history. But what happened a week after the game was equally noteworthy.

Two professors, Albert Hastorf and Hadley Cantril, had Dartmouth and Princeton psychology students who had seen either the game or a film of it fill out a questionnaire about who was at fault and whether the game had been unnecessarily rough and dirty.

When they analyzed the findings, they were surprised to discover that Dartmouth and Princeton students had given completely different responses. Only 36 percent of the Dartmouth students said they felt that Dartmouth had started the rough play; among the Princeton students, a staggering 86 percent said that Dartmouth had instigated the roughness of the game.*

How was this possible? Sure, one would expect a certain number of students to be biased toward their alma mater, but this discrepancy seemed staggering. After all, they had seen the exact same game!

In their published study, Hastorf and Cantril explained it this way: when a person observes different occurrences in the environment, he tends to "select those that have some significance for him from his own ego centric position in the total matrix,"** or in layman's terms, when there is a lot going on around us, we choose to see only the things that we want to see. In other words, the Princeton students saw the details of the game that reinforced their desired view that Dartmouth was at fault for the dirty playing. And the Dartmouth students saw the details that reinforced *their* desired perception that Princeton was to blame.

Of course, this isn't significant just for what it tells us about how we perceive the outcome of college sporting events. What Hastorf and Cantril's discovery teaches us is that we do

---

* Albert H. Hastorf and Hadley Cantril, "They Saw a Game: A Case Study," *The Journal of Abnormal and Social Psychology* 49 (1) (1954).
** Ibid.

not always objectively observe the events of our lives. Rather, we often selectively shape our perceptions of them based on our most deeply held desires and wishes—often without even being aware that we are doing it.

If we're just talking about football games, this does not seem like such a big deal, but what about when it comes to major liminal moments in our lives? When we are deciding whether or not to cross a threshold into a new room, does our selective perception cloud or bias our judgment? Are we making a decision to cross or not to cross based on what we know to be true about what's on the other side or simply based on what we want to believe? Are we aware that our own assumptions and beliefs may be limiting our vision? Can we even distinguish our desires and wishes from reality?

How Does Selective Perception Hurt Us?

Though Hastorf and Cantril didn't coin the term "selective perception" until the midfifties, human beings have had this cognitive bias since the beginning of time. Take, for example, Sarah, the wife of Abraham, who became the father of the Jewish people. Initially, the Bible tells us, Sarah believed she was infertile. In ancient Israel a woman's worth was determined by her ability to bear children, which made Sarah that much more devastated and desperate to have a child. So Sarah beseeched her husband to sleep with Hagar, her maidservant, and bear a child. He did, and they conceived Ishmael.

At first Sarah was pleased. Her husband, too, was thrilled to be a father and have an heir to carry on their lineage. But then the unexpected happened. God appeared to Sarah and told her that she would in fact have a child in her old age. She laughed in disbelief. But nine months later she gave birth to Isaac.

Suddenly, Ishmael was a liability to Sarah, who feared that Abraham would love and favor Ishmael over Isaac. He was, after all, his firstborn, even though she was not his mother. She soon became consumed with jealousy and fear. What if Hagar tried to insist that Ishmael be the couple's sole heir? In biblical times the law stated he had special rights of inheritance, and the firstborn male of the maternal line had even more. Sarah wanted Isaac to be the "firstborn" in order to receive all the privileges of that birthright. She became so focused on Isaac receiving his full inheritance that she could see only one option in front of her: banish both Hagar and Ishmael in the wilderness forever.

However, this rather cruel decision was based on all kinds of assumptions that may or may not have been true. Sarah assumed that Abraham would favor Ishmael. She assumed that Hagar would try to interfere. She assumed that she would someday be forced to make a difficult choice between "her" two children. And with these beliefs firmly embedded in her psyche—despite the lack of any evidence to either confirm or disprove them—she simply couldn't see any other options than to get rid of Hagar and Ishmael.

We can only imagine all the damage she did in that moment to her family and all her relationships. Was Abraham furious at her for banishing the mother of his child and his firstborn? Would he ever forgive her? Did her decision permanently fracture their marriage? And what about Hagar? Obviously they had a relationship if Sarah trusted her enough to allow her to sleep with her husband. It seems likely that in banishing Hagar, Sarah had in effect ended her closest female friendship. And what about Isaac? After seeing his mother act so viciously, was he forever suspicious of her motives? Did he live in fear of her for the rest of his life? With that one rash act, did she shatter the trust of everyone around her?

What if Sarah had not been so biased by her selective perception? Would the boys have grown up together as true brothers? Would Hagar have been there to help her weather the later hardships of her own life? Would her husband have loved her even more for her compassion and understanding?

We will never know what could have been because Sarah was so blinded by her desire for Isaac to be the firstborn that she saw only the evidence that confirmed her existing beliefs, and she ignored everything else.

All too often we behave just like Sarah. We become so singularly focused on getting to a particular room, our vision narrows to include only that one room, blinding us to everything else. As a result, we fail to see so many other rooms—so many other great opportunities, experiences, and paths toward happiness—right in front of our faces.

Part of the reason we cannot see the way to other rooms is the simple fact that our perceptions and ideas about the world are so deeply embedded. To perceive literally means to know or identify by means of the senses. As a result, our perceptions of the next room are subjective, not objective, because, as was the case for those football fans, we are so biased by what we *wish* the reality to be. We desperately want the relationship to work out; therefore we ignore that he says he just wants to be friends and only calls late at night to hang out. We desperately want to live on our own, so we move into a nasty roommate situation believing that our presence will change it.

Often our subjective view can be so powerful that we actually believe we are being objective. And the more convinced we become that we are being objective when we are not, the more the voice of reason gets quashed by the voice of our emotions, making it even harder for us to give up our preconceived notions because to us they are the truth.

Making things harder still, these preconceived notions are often instilled in us during the susceptible years of childhood, when all kinds of outside influences—our parents, our teachers, how and where we are raised—can permanently and powerfully shape how we think about the world and can prevent us from even believing there are more options in the world.

Many of us were conditioned to believe that we had to meet certain goals by a certain age or our lives would be over.

Be married by twenty-five, have a child by thirty, and reach career success by forty. And we believed that if we doggedly pursued these goals, then we would achieve them regardless. Alongside our parents the media would reinforce these messages, reminding us that these were our only choices, and if we did not achieve them, then we were a failure.

Often I meet with children who have been programmed their entire lives. From early on they were given a very clear script of where to go and what to do. All they had to do was obey the rules, work hard, and hit these markers. So they did as they were told without ever realizing that there were other ways to live. They got the grades. They did the activities. They fulfilled all of what was expected of them and they believed that as long as they worked hard and continued on this path—each time they entered a new room—they would enjoy a life exactly like the one that their parents had promised them.

When I met with Kevin, he was in a terrible state. He had gone to Yale, worked on Wall Street, and was headed exactly where he was "supposed to" go. But when his fiancée dumped him at twenty-nine, he was crushed beyond repair. He had so bought the false idea that you should continue blindly and resolutely toward your goal that he had never stopped to think about whether it was even what he wanted. It was not that he had decided not to entertain the possibility of other rooms; he didn't even know that they existed. No one had ever told him that he could detour from the script—

or rewrite it altogether. No one had ever told him that there were other rooms that would lead to opportunities, so it's no surprise that he truly believed there were no other options in the world. So when his fiancée dumped him, he thought his life was over.

These messages aren't usually communicated directly or explicitly; more often we absorb them from what we see around us. When Alexis was a child, for instance, her parents argued all the time. Understandably, she was deeply troubled by it and vowed that if she married, she would never argue with her spouse, ever. She would have a peaceful marriage no matter what. That was her single goal for her marriage; nothing else mattered. Eventually she met Evan and they dated for about a year. There was nothing really to argue about, and they never did. After thirteen years of marriage and two kids, they had issues, as everyone would. Except Alexis had vowed never to argue. So instead of communicating her frustrations to Evan, she would bury them. But with no outlet for her frustration, over time she became more and more resentful of him. And he became more resentful of her because he wasn't able to raise issues that they needed to discuss for fear of upsetting her.

Eventually, they got to a point where they were constantly tiptoeing around each other. Ironically, she had been so vested in keeping the peace and never arguing that she was pushing them further and further apart and creating even more problems. She became so blinded by her desire for marital harmony that she could not even see that she was pushing her husband away. She could not see that she was often frustrated and angry with him and as a result shorter-tempered with her children. She could not see that unknowingly she was modeling for her children a troubled marriage—albeit troubled in a different way—just as had been modeled for her as a child.

When I first suggested to Alexis that her myopic focus on keeping the peace was damaging her marriage, she did not understand. She was still so focused on not replicating her parents' problem that she was unable to see beyond that narrow field of vision. But in time I helped her see that while a healthy marriage was not necessarily one in which you argued all the time, it was not necessarily one in which you never argued, either. In time she was able to see that a healthy marriage might be one in which you confront difficult conversations, even if sometimes you argue because you want an honest relationship rather than a pretend "peaceful" one.

This tendency to become so focused on a single desired outcome in our lives that we become blind to everything else doesn't manifest itself just in our personal relationships but in our professional lives as well. Many of us have had the experience of being so focused on achieving one goal or reaching one milestone or grasping one opportunity in our careers that we completely miss all the other excellent goals, milestones, and opportunities right in front of us.

When I lecture to companies, at the end of my presentation I am invariably asked about the two-faced employee. This is the employee who is so determined to get promoted that she is singularly focused on one thing and one thing only: impressing the boss. When she is with the boss, she could not be nicer. But the second the boss is out of the room, that agreeableness and generosity instantly disappear and her alter ego takes over. She feels threatened, and as a result treats everyone terribly. In her obsession with impressing the boss, she totally ignores all the other relationships in her office.

What she fails to see is that the people she is treating poorly may actually have significant influence on people whom she is trying to impress. In her shortsightedness she thinks being nice to the boss's assistant or the receptionist won't get her any closer to the promotion, so why bother? But she could not be more wrong.

I once witnessed a situation like this firsthand. When I was putting myself through college, I quickly realized that the on-campus jobs were not the best paying. So I found a job at Chicago's ZS Associates, a successful consulting firm started by two Northwestern finance professors that at the time had over 150 employees. ZS needed an off-hours receptionist to answer the phones, which worked perfectly with my class schedule. And in those early- and late-shift hours, like the doorman of a New York building, I saw everything. I learned who came in early and who stayed late, who was having interoffice relationships, who was brownnosing the boss, and who was slacking off. Some employees I knew by name, as they always talked to me, but others walked by me day after day never saying a word. Of course, I watched but never said anything to anyone. I was the receptionist and my job was to answer the phones.

Until this one night. The firm's owners had crazy schedules teaching, consulting, and traveling, so they frequently met on off hours to discuss the business. Usually these meetings were conducted behind the closed doors of their offices, but on this one night, they came to my desk. Of course, my first thought was that I was in trouble, but that was not it at all. They simply wanted to know what I thought about their employees. At first I demurred. What did I know? I was just the receptionist.

But they had a feeling I knew a lot, and as I began to share with them who was kind, helpful, genuine and who was not, I realized that I knew their employees in a way that they never could. They were looking to me to provide the information to help them build a company filled with people of integrity.

That experience taught me a lifelong lesson (beyond just to be nice to receptionists). It taught me that everyone who thought the way to the promotion was simply to butter up the boss was sorely mistaken. There are a lot of roads to a promotion, and if you focus only on that single one—making nice with the boss—you'll end up missing out on all the rest. There is no one way to a desired outcome, no matter how much you believe that there is.

Do We Really Understand That Fame and Wealth Do Not Equal Happiness?

Every day we are bombarded with messages from the media telling us how to be successful and happy. The daytime talk shows offer us an endless cycle of "experts" peddling helpful hints and tips on how to lead a life of health, wealth, and fulfillment. Countless books lining the shelves of our local bookstores promise us the five steps to spiritual enlightenment or the ten steps to a lifetime of riches. The shiny celebrity faces smiling up at us from the pages of *People* magazine scream that a cool job, toned abs, and a wealthy celebrity boyfriend are the keys to a happy existence.

And each week, as we turn to these magazines, these books, these talk shows to escape our daily stresses and turn off our hyperactive brains, we are repeatedly being bombarded with the exact same messages again and again. If we are rich, famous, invincible, and thin, then we will be happy. And even though on an intellectual level we see the lives of so many celebrities crashing before our eyes, there is a big part of us that internalizes these messages nonetheless. There is still a piece of us that believes that our normal, mundane lives will not bring true happiness; we believe that there is one elusive room out there that holds the secret to happiness, and we become consumed with the desire to get there.

Take Crystal, for example. When I met her, she could not understand why she was not happy. As a child growing up in a small farm town in North Dakota, she used to dream of the "happily ever after." Her mother used to tell her again and again that once she became wealthy, thin, and famous, she would be happy. And so she pursued that path in earnest. She moved to New York, worked as a model, had her nose fixed and teeth veneered. She found some fleeting fame on a reality show and met her husband. So by all accounts she expected to be happy—after all, she had held up her end of the deal. She came to me because she wasn't happy, and she felt duped and cheated.

I explained to Crystal that her strategy of defining happiness in such a narrow and superficial way was preventing her from seeing what authentically made her happy. She was assuming that if she found that one perfect room—the one filled with fame and wealth—she would be fulfilled, just as her mother and the magazines claimed. I asked Crystal about the last time she had felt truly happy. It took her a while to answer, but eventually she shared that it had been at Christmas when she was on the farm with her family. Only then did she realize that it did not matter how much money or notoriety she attained; what mattered was that she feel connected to the people who loved her for her.

Her confusion is understandable. As a society, one of our most entrenched collective assumptions is the notion that wealth will bring us happiness. Yet the data proves otherwise. Of course, if you are living in abject poverty, your happiness is linked to your wealth because you lack money to satisfy your basic needs like food, rest, shelter, and health care. But for most of us who have these basic needs met, material wealth does not correlate with happiness. A case in point is the famous study at Princeton University that proved empirically, in a survey of 450,000 Americans conducted in 2008 and 2009, that once we reach earnings of $75,000 per year, our day-to-day happiness does not rise even if our income does.

David Myers, the author of *The Pursuit of Happiness: Who Is Happy, and Why?*, writes, "Since 1957, the number of Americans who say they are 'very happy' has declined from 35 to 32 percent. Meanwhile, the divorce rate has doubled, the teen suicide rate has nearly tripled, the violent crime rate has nearly quadrupled (even after the recent decline) and more people than ever (especially teens and young adults) are depressed."* But even with this information it is still much easier to adopt the media's oversimplified definition of happiness and success than to define it for ourselves.

The thought of determining for ourselves what actually makes us happy or successful is daunting because it forces us to confront the scary possibility of not being like everyone else. We all want to *believe* that we are nonconformists. But the truth is that our nature is to conform, to fit in, and to be like everyone else. We fear that if we suddenly say that our

---

* David G. Myers, *The Pursuit of Happiness: Who Is Happy, and Why?* (New York: William Morrow & Company, 1992).

definition of happiness is different from someone else's, they might judge us or not like us or possibly even feel rejected by us. Often even when we have no intention at all of putting another person down, they still feel rejected when we make choices for our happiness that are not consistent with theirs.

I counsel mothers all the time who struggle to make sense of their daughters' choices. Rather than see that their daughters may have different paths to happiness, they criticize them endlessly. I think this is because deep down they believe that in choosing another path their daughters are actively rejecting them and the choices that they made as mothers.

Every time I see Sarah, for example, the first thing she always tells me is how her daughters could not possibly be happy and how troubling this is to her. She says, "After all, one lives in Utah, of all places, in a tiny house in a remote part of town with her husband and those dogs, and the other is a local librarian in a public school who has never married. How could they be happy? It is entirely different from how they were raised, in urban Los Angeles with all the fabulous things and privileges that we gave them."

The irony is that I have met both of her daughters many times and they seem truly happy. They love the lives they have constructed for themselves for the past twenty-five years! And even though their adult lives look entirely different from their urban, fast-paced childhood, those lives work for them. However, what makes them unhappy is the constant tension they feel around their mother—that even after all these years, rather than accept and embrace their choices, she still acts as though her daughters are actively condemning the way she raised them simply because they are not making the same choices she did.

When the daughters are with their mother, they spend a tremendous amount of time trying to protect her feelings and get along. So they affirm over and over again that even though their choices are different, they are not a condemnation of hers. And at the same time they try not to feel guilty for their choices. And they try to not cave in to the old notions of happiness that they were prescribed. By the end of a week's visit, the daughters often lament how ready they are to return home because they are exhausted emotionally.

No one likes to spend their emotional time and energy defending their choices and affirming the choices of others to protect their feelings. No one likes to feel judged year after year. So unfortunately, we often opt to simply conform to others' definitions of happiness just to avoid all this emotional work.

In the 1950s the psychologist Solomon Asch demonstrated this powerfully with a series of experiments he conducted to determine to what degree we alter our beliefs and perceptions to conform to the group.* In these clever experi-

---

* Solomon E. Asch, "Studies of Independence and Conformity: A Minority of One Against a Unanimous Majority," *Psychological Monographs: General and Applied* 70 (1956).

ments, he showed individual participants a line segment and then asked them to choose the matching line from three line segments of different lengths. When the individuals were asked to write down the correct match without any knowledge of their peers' answers, 98 percent of the time they chose the correct answer. However, then Asch played a little trick. This time he put the participants into a group setting where one person, planted by Asch, would at first answer correctly but eventually change his response to be incorrect. Then Asch asked the same participants to choose the matching line segment again. This time the results were astonishing. The participants conformed to the incorrect group answer approximately one third of the time. And what's more, the larger the group, the greater the tendency for participants to go along with the answer the others had chosen, even when they knew it to be incorrect. When asked why they'd chosen the answer they did, most participants stated that they knew the answer was wrong, but they just didn't want to appear foolish by going against the grain.

It is often this same fear of looking foolish that causes us to cling to narrow and preconceived ideas of what will bring us success or happiness. Kathleen, for example, was married for twenty-eight years but was very unhappy. Her husband was not a bad man, but they had stopped being intimate years earlier and she craved love and connection. After trying for years to change their marriage and begging him to go to therapy (which he refused), she had reached a point where she knew something had to give, but she was conflicted about what to do.

When I met her at this liminal moment, it was clear to me that her life did not make her happy. And it hadn't for a long time. But what was not clear to me was whether she was going to do anything about it. She did not want to be a divorcée. She did not want to be the single one among all her married friends. She was terrified of the possible humiliation—the judgmental looks, the pitying stares.

And she was also terrified to redefine her own image of herself. She had always seen herself as the woman who is married. The one who stays through thick and thin. The one who never leaves. She was so blinded by her need to stay in that room so she could uphold that "perfect" image of herself, she simply couldn't see the other, much better, rooms available to her.

I explained to Kathleen that there were no guarantees that if she left her marriage, she would automatically be happy. But if she *did* leave her marriage, even though that meant facing the discomfort of possibly looking foolish, she upped her chances significantly.

Three years later I ran into Kathleen and she looked truly happy. I assumed that she had left her marriage and found a new love. It turned out I was wrong, but I was also right. I was right that she had gotten a divorce. But I was wrong to think that it had immediately made her happier. To the contrary, the year she left her husband had been the "worst year of [her] life." Everything that happened had confirmed her worst fears. Most of her couple friends abandoned her. Her children were angry with her. She second-guessed herself again and again. Many days she regretted her decision. She thought constantly about going back to him.

But eventually she got an apartment. She found a job working in a department store. She started dating, no one in particular. She hadn't fallen in love again, as she had hoped, and she was not exuberantly happy, but most days she was fine. One day, when she was selling cosmetics, her ex-husband walked up to the counter. They started chatting. She told him about her new life and he shared details of his own. After Kathleen had left, he had decided to take stock and finally go to a therapist. He had realized that he too was unhappy, and he had begun to understand her decision to leave.

After about an hour of talking, he asked her to drinks. Soon they began dating. All of her friends thought this was a terrible idea and tried to convince her to break it off. But she didn't, and to her surprise, they fell in love again.

When I ran into her she told me that when she had sat in my office three years prior, she never could have imagined that this would happen. Who could have? But that is what made her story so compelling to me. Leaving him did not lead her exactly where she *thought* she wanted to go. Who would have thought, at the time of her divorce, that getting back together with her husband would even be a viable option? But the very act of crossing the threshold had broadened her field of vision, allowing her to see possibilities for happiness that she'd never imagined. And as a result she ended up discovering the love and happiness she was seeking in a way she could never have anticipated. If he had not literally come up to her and asked her out again, it never would have occurred to her that it was an option, let alone the right one.

On the surface Kathleen's story seems unique. I mean, how many people actually reunite with their ex-husband? But at its core her story is all of our stories. Most of our decisions do not lead us exactly where we want to go. Yet the more narrowly focused we are on a particular destination—the more focused we are on getting to a particular room—the harder it can be to see the alternatives. After all, if you've spent half your life chasing a dream—whether a dream job, a dream marriage, or a dream family—it's terrifying to suddenly switch course and take a chance on something different. Yet only once we broaden our scope of vision can we see all the many other possibilities for happiness. As Edward Albee writes in his play *The Zoo Story,* "Sometimes you have to go a long way out of your way to come back a short distance correctly."

How Do We Open Up Our Field of Vision?

The first step in opening up our field of vision to see the possibilities we might otherwise have missed is to realize that we can never be totally free of our biases. But we can become far more aware of them—both the conscious and the unconscious ones. We can learn to open our eyes to the fact that there are *always* other ways and other paths.

It helps to get a variety of perspectives, not just from people we trust but also from people who have no vested interest—neutral parties. Often neutral third parties can see things in ways that we have never entertained or even imagined. It is far easier to question our preconceived ideas when prompted by someone whom we respect but who has no agenda about the path we take.

There is a popular experiment often taught in entry-level psychology in which two people are shown identical images of a woman, then are asked if the woman is young or old. Virtually every time this experiment is conducted, some students say they saw an old woman and others say they saw a young woman. In reality the image is an optical illusion; the picture could be of a young or an old woman, depending on how you look at it. Interestingly, only once the participants are told that the image contains *both* an old and a young woman are they able to see both women in the picture. Sometimes all we need is someone else to remind us that there are other ways of interpreting the world—if we can just learn to look at things a little differently.

Sometimes distracting our minds with some idea or activity entirely unrelated to the decision at hand helps divert us from our preconceived notions. It's human nature to obsess about or overanalyze important decisions, particularly at liminal moments. But paradoxically, the more we obsess, the more we convince ourselves that our original idea is the only option; we carve a deep neural groove that makes it difficult to think in any other way. When we distract ourselves with something that is entirely unconnected to the threshold we are crossing—maybe an activity like yoga or reading a book—we activate new neurons and open up pathways in our brains that enable us to entertain other choices.

The final step is to get uncomfortable. I know, I know. Who wants to be uncomfortable? But often it's only once we leave our comfort zone and become willing to try something new that we open up possibilities and options that we never knew we had.

We spend so much of our time trying to get to the rooms that feel safe. But maybe it is time for us to focus our energy on getting comfortable with being uncomfortable. After all, just the act of putting ourselves in an uncomfortable position without doing a thing is a change. Maybe forcing ourselves to enter those "unsafe" rooms even when—or *especially* when—it makes us uncomfortable can help us grow in ways that we never anticipated.

Often people come to me for advice because they want to get married but are having trouble meeting the right person. I counsel them to try online dating. I don't have hard and fast statistics, but I'd say that about two thirds of the couples I marry meet online. Yet whenever I recommend this to people, I get so much push-back. I hear "But online dating is for desperate people" or "I promised myself I would never online date" or "Online dating is too public. I don't want to be vulnerable to all those people. I don't want my profile on display."

I tell them that, yes, they may feel all those things, but it is important to get comfortable with those discomforts anyway—not only because getting comfortable with these discomforts will increase their chances of finding a spouse but also because it is likely that this is not the only time that they will feel vulnerable, so they might as well try to get accustomed. After all, being in a relationship requires tremendous vulnerability and discomfort, so if the end goal is to be married, I tell them, now would be a good time to start. When we step out of our comfort zone, we not only possibly open up new opportunities but we also develop important life skills that can be learned only through practice and experience.

Some people are afraid to look vulnerable to others. Don't be! You might think vulnerability makes you look weak, but to the contrary: I always admire people who reach out to me to tell me that they are looking for a job or a date. People respect the person who is willing to put himself or herself out there, to open up. It doesn't make you look weak, simply human.

I am not suggesting that you martyr yourself in discomfort. Nor am I suggesting you do something drastic and crazy. Often the greatest opportunity for growth comes when we feel a little bit unsafe. So many people I counsel are scared to try this method because they are sure that if they feel discomfort, they will end up acting in self-destructive ways (like overeating or binge drinking) to try to escape their feelings. They believe those behaviors will then consume their lives, and they will live forever as a miserable person. But what they fail to realize is that as much as we have the option to turn to destructive behaviors in times of discomfort, we also have the option to turn to constructive ones.

I often remind people that when we feel shaky we can easily turn to adaptive behaviors to comfort ourselves rather than maladaptive ones. When you are struggling in one area of your life, there is no shame in seeking out comfort in another. When you are struggling with your work environment, spend more time focusing on your home one. If you are having trouble in a romantic relationship, lean on your friends for extra support. Often we forget how many places and people really want to provide us with comfort if we actually turn to them. But we have to know who and what they are before we become so disoriented that we cannot identify them.

Seek out people who can truly be with you in your discomfort. All too often I see people judge their friendships based on who was a better friend to them when they were in pain and discomfort. I actually advise people against assessing their friends during difficult times. Some people are more equipped to be with others when they are in pain and some people are less equipped. Some friends will see you suffer and want to rush in with a fire extinguisher and fix the problem, while others can just be with you and hold your hand. It is not that one friend is better than the other; it is just that each one of us handles suffering differently. It's up to you to determine who will provide you with the most comfort.

Similarly, it is worthwhile to notice which environments give you the most comfort. You may feel more at peace in a cabin in the woods or a noisy urban restaurant. Some people find solace in the ongoing din at a crowded Starbucks while others just find it really hectic. Like friends, one environment might be more comforting to you at certain times than others; it's not about better or worse, just different. Knowing places that give you solace and spending more time in them when you are struggling can enable you to cope better with the discomfort.

If all this talk of discomfort sounds unpleasant or daunting, consider the fact that the people we most admire in life are the people who take the most chances, who follow the least "safe" path. We endlessly retell stories, for example, of the person who left his high-paying career to follow his passion to become a teacher and now travels to third-world countries to educate those in need. But when we tell those stories we fail to retell all the uncomfortable stuff that happened in between. We don't mention how his wife resented him for changing their lifestyle and how he had to tolerate her resentment day after day. We don't talk about how hard it was for his children when he was away from home. We don't talk about all the times he doubted himself, regretted his decision, and felt like a failure.

Maybe that is the problem. We get so overly focused on

the end result that we blind ourselves to the fact that the road isn't always smooth and easy; we see only the happy end result we want to see and ignore all the trials and tribulations along the way. We congratulate people for taking the risk and getting the reward. But maybe what we should really admire in those people is the struggle that they went through. Maybe we should spend more time talking about all bumps in the road—rather than just the end of the journey.

I remember a very successful actor once being interviewed on a morning show. He looked very young, but he was actually in his late thirties. The interviewer turned to him and said, "How are you handling all this success and fame since it happened so quickly?" He looked at her, truly confused. Then he said, "My success did not happen quickly at all. It has been twenty years of being rejected at auditions, waiting tables, and enduring the criticism of my family and my own identity." The interviewer seemed as shocked as I was to hear him say that, live on television in front of millions of viewers. That's because no one talks about the gory details of the journey.

When we tell our stories to others, we want them to sound effortless. We want to appear as if it all came easily to us—as if we simply picked the destination we wanted to reach or the goal we wanted to achieve, pursued it doggedly and unwaveringly, and eventually succeeded. But in real life it never happens like this. There are always false starts, detours, and course corrections, and more often than not the room we end up in is not the one we first envisioned. Maybe if we begin to tell our stories differently, if we start to talk about all the times our journey didn't go as smoothly as expected, we can help others look past their preconceived notion that the road to the "perfect" room is without speed bumps and glitches.

What if we started talking about how we continued to question our assumptions and beliefs about what rooms were "right"? What if we started to narrate all the times we opened up our field of vision to see *all* the rooms in front of us, around us, and even unknown to us because we did not conform to someone else's ideas or even to our own ideas of what happiness looks like?

Then we would be authentic and honest. Wouldn't those qualities be the most inspiring to us?

Now I understand why every high school student must read Robert Frost's "The Road Not Taken." Our tendency is to follow the road that everyone takes. But when we do, we lose sight of all the other roads that could have led elsewhere. We start to believe this is the best road and the right road because it is the one to which we have grown so accustomed. When I was in high school, I thought we all must read it because we were being encouraged to take the less traveled path. But I had it wrong. What Frost teaches is that we'll never really know which road is the right one: "Two roads diverged in a wood, and I—I took the one less traveled by, and that has made all the difference." Frost does not claim that taking the road less traveled was better, or even that it led him to where he wanted to go. It was just different.

In Judaism there is a series of blessings that you say as you wake up each morning. Each one corresponds to a particular action. For example, as you open your eyes, you say the blessing "Thank you, God, for allowing me to open my eyes." This one can be taken very literally, and I imagine many people do and perform it purely perfunctorily. But I believe that the liturgists wrote it with a deeper meaning in mind. When we wake up each morning, we are supposed to open our eyes anew. Each day when you wake up, try to see this day without bringing to it all the preconceived ideas and notions that you had before. Judaism is saying, "Open your eyes." Because if you don't, then you will not be able to see all the other rooms around you.

If we want to make the most of this journey we call life, we need to remind ourselves of this message over and over again. We need to remember to open our eyes and look for those other, less traveled roads because they may lead us to places far better than we ever expected. As Thomas H. Huxley, the famous scientist, put it, we must "be prepared to give up every preconceived notion, follow humbly wherever or to whatever abysses nature leads, or [we] shall learn nothing."*

---

* T. H. Huxley, *Letters and Diary 1860*.

Chapter 6

Backward Is Not an Option

You can't start the next chapter of your life if you keep re-reading the last one.

—unknown

On the very last page of my first book, *We Plan, God Laughs,* I wrote, "I am not sure how it all ends for me, for my mother, for you. God does not know either." When the book was published, my mother was perfectly healthy. So as I wrote those words I imagined that she would live well into her nineties, just as her mother had. Since she was only sixty at the time, I believed that we had another thirty years together.

So you can imagine that I was devastated—as were my stepfather and brother—to learn only a year later that she had terminal brain cancer. She endured eighteen months of dispiriting doctors' appointments, painful chemotherapy and radiation, and complete and utter deterioration as the disease ravaged her body. Finally, when her body could endure no more, she took her last breaths around 6:30 a.m. on April 25, 2010, as I held her hand, whispered "I love you" in her ear, and let her go.

When she was dying, I had only one desire: to be constantly by her side. Everyone who had claims on my time—my four children, my husband, my congregants, my agent, my editor—in my mind had to wait. And they did. They knew that her time was limited and that when she died, I would return to being the person I had once been. I would resume driving carpool and correcting homework. I would start to officiate weddings and funerals again. I would complete my second book. I would go on date night. And I reassured them again and again that my absence was temporary. I would come back and be the mother, the rabbi, the writer, the wife that I had once been.

But once she died, and even after the shivah (the seven-day period of mourning) and the *shloshim* (the thirty-day period of mourning) ended, I felt worse, not better. I had thought that I had done most of my grieving as she was dying and that once the inevitable happened, I would start to return to myself again. But as time wore on, the grief became more and more consuming. Rather than returning to who I had once been, I was instead becoming someone entirely different than I had ever been. And as the months went by, all the people who had waited so patiently were becoming less and less understanding.

I could not explain what was happening to me, as I did

not understand it myself. I had always been the person who could bounce back. When a boy broke up with me, I got over him quickly. When a friend disappointed me, I moved on and I became stronger. When I hit a professional roadblock, I found a new road. But this time I was not bouncing back. All I wanted to do was sleep, look at pictures of my mother, and reminisce about how great our life had been before she got sick, before she died. I had no motivation professionally or personally. I did not want to socialize. I did not want to work. I did not even want to be with my children. I was depressed, paralyzed by my grief.

It became apparent to me that I was in a hallway I had never been in before. That I, the person who helped people get unstuck and move forward across the thresholds of their lives, was in fact very stuck, unable to move in any direction.

As you can imagine, all the people who cared for me and had dreams for me were beyond worried. They each had different suggestions for how to help me: therapy, medication, and exercise. They even resorted to veiled threats. "You are going to destroy your career, your marriage, and your children if you don't get your act together." I knew they were right and I tried to follow their suggestions, but all of my attempts were halfhearted. What I really wanted was to return to the way things were. I wanted to go back to the life in which my mother was well and everything was how I (falsely) remembered it—*perfect*.

But over time the hallway darkened even more because I

slowly began to realize that of course I could never go back. It was not just that my mother had died; it was that the person I had been before she got sick had also died. All of the experiences of the past few years—learning of her diagnosis, taking care of all her needs, burying her, grieving her—had changed me. I was no longer the person I had been before. And I could never revert back to that person or that life no matter how badly I wanted to. I slowly began to understand that if I wanted *any* life, then I had to accept what had happened and begin to take steps to move forward to a new room and start a new chapter, even if I did not want to.

So I began to ask myself, *How do we accept that we cannot go back? How do we move forward when all we want to do is move backward? How do we find the courage to believe that there is another room in front of us if we move toward it?*

And so I began to write. I began to teach. I began to volunteer. I began to take small steps across the threshold toward a new room and a new life with a new me.

Use the Past to Propel You Forward

When we experience some traumatic change in our life—whether it's the passing of a parent, a painful divorce, or, God forbid, the death of a child—as much as we might yearn to go back to the way things once were, it is impossible. What was behind us no longer exists as we knew it, not because it changed but rather because *we* changed. It's kind of like how the house you grew up in did not get smaller; you got bigger. What happened in the past changed who you are, and now you cannot return to that old you because that you no longer exists.

This is a painful truth to accept, especially when we are in a dark hallway, scared and unsure of what lies ahead. When we are stricken with doubts and fears about the future, our brains reflexively tell us that the past was better; and whether this is true or not, our tendency is to believe it. So it is understandable that instead of running forward to the unknown our instinct is to run backward, toward what is known: the past.

Making matters worse is the fact that we as humans are actually wired with a tendency to romanticize the past, to remember it as better than it actually was. When researchers from Johns Hopkins University set out to uncover why, they discovered that each time we recall a memory, different neurons in our hippocampus and cortex—where memories are stored—are activated and that "every reactivation re-encodes the memory, and depending on what cortical neurons are engaged, can strengthen, weaken or update particular memory features."* In other words, our brains remember our past

---

* Emilie Reas, "Important New Theory Explains Where Old Memories Go," *Scientific American* (October 2013).

differently each time we reflect on it, and each time we remember the past favorably, our brains actually recode that memory, strengthening the favorable details and emotions associated with the memory. Essentially, "our memories are transformed each time we revisit them."*

Researchers also found that our brain tends to strengthen the positive memories and weaken the negative ones, so much so that over time some of our most difficult and painful memories are erased entirely. Psychologists believe this is because our brains are protecting us from pain, unconsciously. That's why many people who have suffered serious trauma cannot remember anything about it. Their brains are motivated to forget and block the anxiety-arousing memories. It is an adaptive mechanism that nature has designed to prevent them from being paralyzed by what happened in the past and allow them to continue to move forward in their lives.

But even in those of us who have not suffered serious trauma, the brain works in similar ways. Scientists actually call this phenomenon the "doorway effect." Gabriel Radvansky, Sabine Krawietz, and Andrea Tamplin studied the reason why we walk to our bedroom to grab a coat but by the time we get there, we forget completely why we went there in the first place. Most of us think that we are just being forgetful, or that we are not being present enough, but the researchers found there was another reason. They asked a group of

* Ibid.

participants to look at a recognizable object and then put it in a shoebox so they could not see what it was. They then had the participants carry the shoebox a certain distance within the same room and asked them to identify without looking what object was in the box. Next, they asked the participants to walk the same distance, but this time by passing through a doorway. Even when the distance was the same, the participants' memory and ability to recall what was in the shoebox was significantly slower and less accurate when they passed through a doorway than when they did not. In other words, just the act of walking through a doorway caused more forgetting (interestingly, the researchers also discovered that the doorway did not even have to be an actual one; they arrived at the same results when the participants were tested using a virtual doorway within a video game). The researchers concluded that "walking through a doorway is a good time to purge your event models because whatever happened in the old room is likely to become less relevant now that you have changed venues. That thing in the box? Oh, that is from what I was doing *before* I got here; we can forget all about that."* And they did.

What these findings tell us is that whenever we cross a threshold, real or metaphorical, it signals to our brain to forget what came before. That's why we so easily remember all

---

* C. B. Brenner and J. M. Zacks, "Why Walking Through Doorway Makes You Forget," *Scientific American* (December 2011).

the fun of the summer at the beach but forget the bugs, the heat, and all the complaining. We remember the joy of giving birth but we forget the pain (well, at least the extent of the pain), the bleeding, the stitches (I know I would not have had four children if I remembered every single aspect of giving birth!).

So you can see how the brain makes it easy to romanticize the past. Those were "the good old days." When we say those words, they transport us back to another time. Often our present is painful and the future is unknown. By waxing nostalgic we can be there, not here. *When I was a child, I did not have a care in the world. When I was single, I had freedom and independence. When I worked for that company, I was respected and valued.* And so on.

When Christy saw on Facebook that Max, her ex-fiancé, was now divorced, she sent him a message. He replied right away, and immediately they made plans to meet for an innocent coffee to catch up. She met him one afternoon and they had a pleasant time reminiscing about their college relationship. However, once she got home, even though she was happily married, she could not stop thinking about "what could have been." Had she married Max, how would her life have been different? Would it have been better? Should she have married him instead of her husband? Had she made a mistake?

She came to me because she could not stop obsessing

over these questions. I asked her to think about all the reasons that she had decided not to marry him. "We were young. He was unfocused. He was a bit of a player. I worried that he would not be faithful." As soon as she started to remember these concerns, her feelings began to change. Later she learned that her instincts had been right: he had cheated on his wife and he did have issues with loyalty. But it was only once she forced herself to remember the not-so-good feelings of her past with him that she was able to leave her romanticized notions of him behind.

We also have a bias toward remembering what we *want* to remember. Consciously we know everything was not always perfect. But subconsciously we reconstruct the memories to reflect the way we wish to narrate our story. Eventually our retelling becomes our truth. We may not have walked five miles in the freezing snow, but after telling that story again and again, we actually believe we did. Some parts of those statements may be true, but the likelihood is that they tell only part of the reality. As Elie Wiesel says, "Some stories are true that never happened."*

You may have had a wonderful childhood, but no matter how good it was, growing up is hard for most everyone, and you probably struggled like everyone else. Likewise, you may

* Gary Weissman, *Fantasies of Witnessing: Postwar Efforts to Experience the Holocaust* (New York: Cornell University Press), 67–68.

have had freedom while you were single, but there probably were also nights you lay awake worrying that you would be alone for your entire life. When we reflect on the past, it is all too easy to forget the doubts and concerns that we had about our future at the time (after all, if we have doubts about our future now, why not then?), not to mention all our insecurities and our missteps.

The good news is that we use these memories of overcoming past difficulties to propel us forward. We can say to ourselves, *I got through that, so I can get through this.* But this is a mind-set that doesn't always come naturally, especially when we are in the throes of grief and fear. To cultivate it can take some work.

In helping people move through difficult transitions, I often have them list on paper all the difficult transitions that they made in their past. At first they are reluctant to write down anything. They believe that those previous transitions don't really qualify as "difficult"—and indeed, it might seem that way because they are now on the other side of them. In hindsight they think those transitions cannot even compare to the one that they are dealing with now. But once they list them on paper, some of the memories start coming back. That's when I have people identify what tools helped them to cross those thresholds. And to their surprise, more often than not the same tools that they used then are the ones that they need to use now. Yet it is only when I make them see it in black and white that they are able to recognize that their memories of the past can now help them move forward—instead of serving as an excuse not to.

Margaret, for example, came to me because her husband had become a drug addict and she was consumed with worry. She told me that she had never experienced anything like this anxiety and sadness and that she was not sure she could take this pain much longer. When I urged her to write down some of the challenges of her past, she told me that she had had an idyllic childhood and that there was nothing in her past that could compare to what she was feeling. But then she remembered that there was a time when her father had fallen into a deep depression. Her mother had to take over their family business and she as the oldest had to care for her three younger siblings. When I had her think about that time, she remembered how much anxiety and worry she had felt for them and how she had dealt with it. She told me that she had coped by focusing on and taking care of what needed to be done on a daily basis, rather than worrying about the future. She had continually reminded herself that the situation wasn't permanent, as her siblings would get older, as would she, and eventually they would not need her in the same way. And that one day her father might even get better.

She was right. Her siblings got older. Her father got help and her mother resumed her role as mother. Reflecting on that experience years later helped her see that she had tools from her past to cope with her husband's addiction. She began to see that her past was not an idyllic place that she should dream of returning to; rather, it was a place from which she could draw the strength to care for her sick husband and possibly create a new future for her, for him, and for both of them.

It's Not the "What" That's Changed; It's the "Who"

In liminal moments, particularly painful or challenging ones, we don't readily think about how we can use our past to move forward; we think only about how much we wish we were still there. But we must remind ourselves that just as we can never predict exactly how we will feel in the future, we cannot repeat exactly how we felt in the past. We cannot replicate our feelings, no matter how much we want to. Even if we jumped back into the arms of our first love, that first kiss would not feel the same because it would not be the first.

The advent of the Internet and Facebook has made it that much easier for people to revisit and romanticize their past. They are reconnecting with old flames, e-mailing with old friends, and in many cases even revisiting old stomping grounds. And often, after people reconnect with someone whom they have not talked to in years, they find themselves confused. No matter how happy they may be in their current life, after having reconnected with an old someone, old feelings—idyllic memories of first loves, nostalgic recollections of good times with the old gang back in the hometown, happy (if inaccurate) reminiscences of a carefree time before the full range of adult responsibilities took hold—are stirred up. Now they find themselves second-guessing the life choices that they have made and wishing they could relive those feelings by going back to how things once were.

Alternatively, people find each other after a long time and it is not the same at all. In high school there were fireworks, but now there is zero chemistry. After they exchange a few pleasantries back and forth there is really not that much to say. And this too is confusing because it is hard to understand what changed. Back then we could talk for hours, and now talking for a moment feels like hours. But what we often fail to realize is that it's not the *what* that has changed; it's we who have changed. Our lives have changed, our interests have changed, our priorities have changed, and we cannot expect that they will be aligned with the other person's, as theirs have changed too over time.

The point is that life is not like a video game in which you can reset and restart anew or from where you left off. Even when the players look and sound the same, they are not. For better or for worse, time changes all of us.

Think about the experience of seeing a movie for the second time. It is never as good as the first. Obviously the movie did not change; you did. You may still feel emotional when you see the heartbreaking climax, but you will not feel it in the same way as you did before.

With a movie only you (the viewer) change. But in relationships the other person changes as well. Often we underestimate how much we ourselves have changed over time;

gradual changes can be hard to see when we live with ourselves on a day-to-day basis. So when we reconnect with someone from our past, we think, *I am not all that different. How much could that other person have changed?* But we are fooling ourselves. Even if it appears that not much has changed on the outside, we are *all* different people now.

Of course, it becomes that much easier to romanticize who we were in the past when things are not going so well for us in the present. This is what happened to Evan. When he ran into his college sweetheart and "fell madly back in love" during their weekend rendezvous, he told me it was just like they were eighteen again. He and his wife of fifteen years had been struggling for a long time. And she and her husband had been struggling for just as long. Both of their marriages were on the brink, and by "falling madly in love" like they did when they were eighteen, they could justify leaving their respective partners. Within a few weeks, they filed for divorce from their spouses and moved in together.

But they soon learned that life together at forty-five was very different from what it had been at eighteen. For one thing, Ellen now had four kids and lived on the West Coast. Evan had two and lived three thousand miles away. She was a physician with a thriving practice; he was a struggling writer just making ends meet. He wanted more kids; she didn't. They both needed to live geographically close to their ex-spouses because they both shared joint custody. Yet those logistical differences, though considerable, paled in comparison to their personal ones.

Even though they both thought they hadn't really changed, they soon discovered that they in fact had—very much. Ironically, what they had loved most about each other almost three decades ago had become what they most disliked about each other now. Back then she had loved that he was a dreamer. But now she needed a realist to help support their brood. When they were in college, he had loved her drive, but now he felt ignored. As tireless nineteen-year-olds they had had sex every afternoon; now they were too tired to have it even once a week. After a very difficult year of marriage, they realized that no matter how hard they tried, they could not pick back up where they had left off in college; they both had changed too dramatically, whether they acknowledged it or not. They divorced a short time later.

Over and over again, I see people astonished to discover how impossible it is to go back to their past lives and pick up right where they left off. According to a recent Pew Research Center Study, 36 percent of young adults between the ages of eighteen and thirty-one are moving back in with their parents. In some cases there is financial necessity, yet this emerging trend can be very difficult for both parents and children because the roles and relationships that existed before can no longer exist in the same way.

When Candace moved back home after graduating from the University of Florida, for example, it was completely different from what she had imagined. She knew *she* was not the same person, but she had never imagined that her parents had changed as well. At first they thought they would continue where they had left off. And immediately they did fall into some old habits: her parents started to parent her again as if she were a teenager, and as a result, she started to regress to that age. But quickly they all realized that that dynamic did not work for them. Her mother did not want to do her laundry, her father did not want to tell her what time to come home at night, and she in turn felt infantilized and stifled. She and her parents soon began to resent each other, and they were not sure what to do.

Short of her moving out, which was not an option because of her finances, the only thing they could do was to learn how to relate to each other as fellow adults rather than as parent and child. They started by establishing new rules for living together, in much the same way that roommates do. Eventually the situation improved because they were no longer trying to re-create the life that once was; rather, they were moving toward a new life together.

It seems that the nature of life is that we can't go back, we can only go forward. When we wish to re-create the past, we are really wishing to go back to a place that no longer exists. Instead we must start building our future by taking small steps to move onward and upward with the knowledge that we are not the same, and the others around us are not either.

The Bible repeats this message many times over. Jacob was not always a great kid. From the time he was in his mother's womb, he struggled with his twin, Esau. Once they were grown, Esau was bigger, hairier, and a more skilled huntsman. Jacob, on the other hand, was quiet and did not like to mess with weapons. One day, when Esau went out to kill food for his father, Jacob stepped into his place by pretending to be him in front of his dying, almost-blind father. It may not sound like a big deal, but in ancient times Jacob's stealing the place of his brother also meant stealing his position and status in life. Of course, when Esau came back and saw what his brother had done, he was furious and vowed to kill his brother. So Jacob fled.

Years later Jacob wanted to reconcile with his brother. He wanted to apologize face to face, so he sent messengers as an olive branch to find out whether his brother was willing to meet him. When the messengers returned, they told Jacob that Esau was approaching—with an army of four hundred men.

Jacob was terrified, assuming that Esau was coming to kill him as he had vowed to do when he was younger. He instructed his men and his family to leave so that they would not be killed. That night he was all alone when an unknown man came to him as he slept "and wrestled with him until the break of dawn." When Jacob awoke, his hip was injured.

Who was this mystery man? Was it Esau's guardian angel trying to weaken Jacob, as some of the rabbis suggest? Was this God or an angel of God trying to force him to stay and see the confrontation through? Or was it Jacob's conscience wrestling with him? The Bible doesn't tell us.

In the past Jacob had run away. But this was no longer the past and he was no longer that Jacob. Instead of running from the man, he faced him head on, just as he was tempted to do with Esau. Finally, when he could take no more beating, Jacob asked the mystery man to bless him. The mystery man replied, "Your name shall no longer be *Jacob* but *Israel,* for you have striven with beings divine and human and you have prevailed."

While we can only guess who the mystery man was—an angel, God, or Jacob's conscience itself—what is clear is that he gave Jacob a new name to symbolize the fact that he had become a new man. He was no longer Jacob, the one who flees from his problems; rather, he was Israel, the one who confronts them.

And he did. Jacob saw Esau coming and bowed low to the ground in front of him as a sign of respect, knowing that Esau might kill him right then and there. But Jacob was not the only one who had matured. Even though Esau's name was the same, the man who had once vowed to kill his brother now ran to greet him, embraced him, and kissed him.

This story reminds us that time changes us all, that even if we think we are certain of how we—and the people around us—will act in a certain situation, we don't really know. We are changed by our past, and we can never underestimate the changes that they have endured as well.

This message is so important in Judaism that the Bible repeats the motif of changing someone's name as they encounter different life experiences. Abram became Abraham and Sarai became Sarah after they each individually encountered God, to make sure it was clear that they had changed in a significant way.

The modern Jewish tradition has even developed a custom of changing one's name after crossing a significant threshold like illness or divorce. The point of the tradition is to emphasize that we have been transformed by our experience, that we have new wisdom about the world and that that wisdom will reframe how we approach our relationships.

One of the most moving moments of my career was when I officiated the name-changing ceremony for a congregant of mine named Beth. Beth had been diagnosed with stage-four terminal breast cancer. Her chances of surviving were slim to none. She tried everything: chemotherapy, clinical trials, and herbal treatments. And she came very near to death many times. Miraculously, after five years, the cancer finally went into remission. She came to me because she wanted a way to commemorate this transformation from someone who had been "this close" to death to someone who now felt she had a new lease on life.

I shared with her the tradition of changing her name, and so one Sunday morning, not long after we had first spoken, we gathered along with ten of her dearest friends and formally changed her name.

"From now on you will no longer be known as Beth, but you will be known as Batya, the daughter of God, for you are truly God's daughter." As I said those words, we all knew that God was cradling her in His arms.

A name in Judaism is more than just a label; it is a reflection of someone's identity and soul during a specific period of time. In the Talmud, Rabbi Eleazer ben Padat says, "One's name has an influence on one's life." But his teaching is also true in the reverse. One's life is reflected by the name that one has.

In Judaism you have a minimum of three names: one that your parents gave you, one that others call you, and one that you make for yourself. This is because Judaism understands that every time you cross a threshold, you will be changed.

So yes. Whether or not you ever actually change your name, you will inevitably be many different people over the course of your life. Rather than hide from that reality, embrace it. Use all the experiences, wisdom, and knowledge the "new you" has amassed to propel yourself *forward* across each new threshold you face, instead of wishing—pointlessly—that you could go back.

Chapter 7

Make Your Own Luck

Courage means feeling fear and doing it anyway.

—unknown

During your life you may have stood at many thresholds not knowing how to move forward—or even whether you should. At those times you may very well have felt despair, confusion, and total paralysis. My hope for you is that from now onward, those days are over. My hope is that now when you stand at the thresholds, you will have a way of thinking, a way of approaching how to move forward in your life. You will have the courage and mind-set that will enable you to make the decision to move to the next room and then the next. And it is my hope that this new approach will not only serve you in dealing with the obvious thresholds, like getting married or having children or starting a new job, but will also help you navigate the more private, less dramatic decisions and thresholds that confront you on a daily basis.

Because the truth is that just as those major decisions

and thresholds can paralyze us, those "smaller" ones can also derail us from moving forward in our lives as well. Sometimes they can even cause *more* turmoil, confusion, and indecision because they are not so easy to talk about with others; we feel justified in calling our best friend at three in the morning after we've learned our husband is having an affair, for example, but we feel silly making such a big deal about something like "Should I speak up to my boss about someone in the office who isn't pulling her weight?" or "Should I enroll my son in basketball camp against his will?"—even though these "minor" decisions may cause us just as much stress. And so we suffer in silence. We obsess and we do nothing because not only do we not know what to do, but we don't know how to even begin to talk about it.

Then we judge ourselves. We berate ourselves for obsessing over such a "small" decision. We criticize ourselves because we perceive this decision as insignificant and unimportant compared to what other people are dealing with. And those actions chip away at our faith in ourselves. And of course, the more we criticize and judge, the worse we feel and the more our self-trust diminishes. And then the cycle repeats until we feel that we are incapable of doing anything.

I saw a couple named Jack and Melody fall into this vicious cycle when they were trying to decide whether to leave their children a sizable inheritance. Obviously, writing a will involved making a lot of difficult decisions that would profoundly affect who their children would become and how they would live their lives. They had to think about whether the promise of a future safety net would help their children struggle less or whether the knowledge that they would eventually come into a windfall would allow them to become lazy and indulgent. But they didn't want to talk to anyone about it because they knew many people did not have their good fortune, and they didn't want to sound crass and spoiled. But the longer they deliberated without a plan, the more difficult the decision became. Their children were getting older, for one thing, but, more important, the longer they waited, the more paralyzed they became because they became more convinced that no decision would be right.

Or take Frank and Louise, who were deciding whether to remove their child from his current school and put him in a special school because of his learning differences. They didn't want to talk about it, nor did they really want to do it. Though he might not be thriving, he was "fine" where he was. He had tutors and tons of extra care after school. And if they pulled him out, then everyone would know that their child was not "normal," that he was different. Or, worse, people would think that they had given up on him, failed him as parents. They would be stigmatized, humiliated. They would have to leave their circle of friends. And what if he didn't thrive at the new school? They didn't know what to do. So they did nothing, other than obsess. Meanwhile, he continued to suffer and so did they.

Another example is Gabby, who was deciding whether

to take an antidepressant or go to therapy for her anxiety and depression. On the one hand, she was suffering, but on the other, she didn't want to become dependent or "labeled" as depressed. So rather than talk to someone about what to do, she suffered daily, too paralyzed to move in any direction. And with each day not only did her depression immobilize her, but so did her diminishing faith in herself.

Yet private, everyday decisions like these don't have to keep us from moving into a new room any more than the big, monumental decisions do. You have the tools to cross *all* the thresholds, major or minor, public or private, in your life. You have the courage and strength to continue to move forward regardless of the decision you face and, as a result, to begin to trust yourself more and then more. And over time you will continue to discover and develop more and more faith in the most important person: you. This is the very reason I wrote this book.

No matter what the threshold in front of you is, it is not insignificant. It may not be a life-or-death decision. (Most things in life are not, even when they feel that way.) But that does not make it any less important. The decision in front of you is very significant. Every decision you make to cross or not cross a threshold, whether it is narrow or wide, affects the next room that you enter. And that in turn affects the next room that you enter and then the next room and on and on.

And while this may sound obvious as you are reading these words, often when we are actually facing the liminal moments, it is anything but. It is easy to forget that sometimes it is the seemingly inconsequential decision that leads you in another direction and takes you somewhere you never imagined. Sometimes it is that "small" decision that changes everything.

Remember, there is no perfect room. There is no perfect outcome. But I am here to tell you that you can get it right.

You get it right every time you face your fears. Every time you think you are a fraud or an impostor, or you think you will make the wrong choice but you take the risk anyway. Every time you still move forward despite your "past mistakes." Every time you make the conscious choice to live your life with courage and faith rather than with fear and panic.

You get it right when you trust yourself. When you realize that while other people can offer you advice and suggestions, the real answer is inside you. When you choose to believe in yourself—even in moments when you feel tremendous doubt. When you realize that each time you face your fears, you are getting better at it; you are becoming more practiced and more skilled. Then you will see that making the decision to move to the next room becomes easier and easier because you value and trust in your own decisions.

You get it right when you realize that you cannot change the circumstances, the people, or the situations, but you can change how you react. And you don't have to react in the same way that you did in the past. When you truly understand that everything around you will change—including your feelings—you will be able to be more thoughtful about how you respond. And in turn your relationships will grow. You will not need to be apologizing left and right. You will become the person you want to be because you will live and act with respect for yourself and for others.

You get it right when you realize that perfect does not exist. This place that we dream about and see in all those neatly packaged movies is fictional. Life is a process of making imperfect decisions based on imperfect options and finding out where they lead you. Sometimes they lead you places that you intended, but other times they don't. Sometimes they work out in the moment, but oftentimes they don't until many years later. But once you really understand that perfection is not a destination, it takes the pressure off. You don't have to reach some arbitrary benchmark that you set for yourself—or that someone else set for you. You can start participating in the present moment rather than wishing you were somewhere else. And this will release you from those outside demands that have been weighing you down and preventing you from being you.

You get it right when you start to see that there are many ways for things to turn out and that if you are only focused on one, you will miss out. When you begin to see that there are as many incredible outcomes as there are paths. When you stop expecting it to be smooth and easy all the time. When you stop perceiving that other people have it easier than you and stop comparing yourself to others. Once you stop envisioning some destination where you think you "ought" to be going, you will finally see all the amazing possibilities and opportunities actually in front of you.

You get it right when you realize that you cannot go back to who you once were. And this is a good thing. You already did that person. Now it is time to be the *new* you. Now it is time to embrace that person you were who got you here. That person is brave. That person is resilient. That person is complex. That person is deserving. You are deserving.

This is why so many people say in hindsight, *Now it all makes sense*. It is not because they made one decision that turned out perfectly—that landed them in the room they wanted to stay in for the rest of their lives. It is because they made a *series* of decisions, and each one led them into a new room. And even when they were sure a room was not where they were supposed to be, or it felt really hard, or they could not imagine it getting better, they did not give up. They realized that they had to keep going forward into the next room and then the next, until they found the one that felt right.

Don't get me wrong. This is not to say that liminal moments are not difficult. I am not saying that you should be walking around with a huge smile on your face after your husband tells you he has a gambling problem or after you have a miscarriage or after a parent dies. These moments suck. And they are painful. And the grief and the sadness will be real and may last for a long time. And you will think then, *I cannot go on*. But what I am here to tell you is that even in those moments when you are sure that the game is up, your life is over, and you can never recover, you are wrong. If you continue to move forward and cross the thresholds in front of you, then one day it *will* all make sense. And you will say, *It was a hard time in my life. I had a lot of pain. I did not want to go on. But that moment, hard as it was, led me to there. And then that led me to here. And I am okay.* And much of the time you will be *more* than okay; you will be better and stronger than you ever thought you could be.

As a rabbi I tell people that God has bigger plans for each one of us than we do for ourselves. And even though many people don't believe in God (or care what plans He may or may not have for them), the sentiment is a comfort nonetheless. It reminds us that our lives are bigger and better than any one person. There is someone or something out there—whether it's God or our own faith in ourselves or the universe—looking out for us.

In my work people are constantly coming to me from a place of total and utter despair. They think that their lives are over. But almost without exception they come back months or years later and tell me a different story. They tell me that their life could not be better.

I'll never forget Jenna, who thought her life was over when her husband left her penniless with three kids. When she came to me, she had no faith in herself. She was sure that she had ruined her kids' lives and that she was worthless.

But she could not see what I saw: a woman bravely facing instead of running from her problems, a woman knowing that the answer was not coming tomorrow or the next day but that one day it might.

Eventually that day came. Years later, when she came to see me again, she was running a successful real estate business. Her children had all graduated from college and were financially and emotionally stable and happy. She was in love with a wonderful widower. And she was much happier than she had ever been in her life. She was able to say these exact words: "It all makes sense now. I am okay. In fact, I am great."

I tell this story and many others like it on a daily basis to remind my clients that no matter what they are facing, they too will be okay. Yet almost every time, when a person is in terrible pain, they doubt the story. They try to convince me that that person is the exception. They tell me that person "got lucky."

It is said that "luck is the residue of design." I heard this quote for the first time from my wise husband, but in fact it was John Milton, most known for his epic poem *Paradise Lost,* who wrote it. To me, Milton is saying that luck happens when you are standing at a threshold and you cross it—not because you know what will happen, not because it will lead you to a certain destination, but because you believe and you trust that someday it will make sense. Milton is saying that people who are persistent and stay the course get lucky *because* they keep going. They make their own luck by choosing to keep crossing the thresholds in front of them.

If you want to get lucky, if you want to be the story that I tell others, find your faith. Others will say that *you* are the exception. But you will know better. You are living a life better and more meaningful than you ever imagined because you trusted in yourself despite the obstacles, the pain, and the disappointments. You had faith when things looked really awful. You had faith in yourself when you thought happiness was impossible. So you kept moving forward, you kept believing in happiness, and soon you experienced the greatest "luck" of all: happiness found *you*.

So cross the threshold in front of you. Don't wait for some "perfect" time or circumstances. Just forge ahead. And even if you are in the depths of grief or confusion or paralysis, know that this is not your destiny. I guarantee that if you keep that faith, you will one day see yourself (and others will see you) not only as lucky but as blessed. And it will not be because the stars aligned or because you made a series of perfect moves; it will be because you had the courage and resilience to keep going until you found the room that was right for you.

Acknowledgments

When I got stuck in a hallway for a while, it was pretty dark and I was not sure this book would ever see the light. Fortunately the faith, encouragement, and love of some very extraordinary people saw me through.

To Mel Berger, my agent, I am lucky to have you in my corner. You are the definition of a mensch. Your talks mean more to me than I could ever convey. You are a wonderful friend.

To Talia Krohn, I have loved working with you. Your talent as an editor is beyond measure. You have shown me that writing can be both seamless and true. I look forward to a lifetime of collaborations.

To Jason Hodes and Michael Palgon, your support and belief in me over the years has sustained me and I wish that I had told you more often.

To Mel and Enid Zuckerman and my Canyon Ranch family, thank you for giving me a home to think, speak, dream, and restore my soul.

To Ira Stone, Mindy Shapiro, Jonathan Jaffe Bernhard, Rachel Bovitz, and Richard Camras, learning Mussar these years with you has made me understand what it means to serve the other. You walk the walk.

To Gordon Tucker, from our first meeting at my rabbinical school interview until today, you have never let me stray intellectually, emotionally, or professionally. When others doubt, your belief in me never wavers.

To Eddie Feinstein, you are a rabbi's rabbi. Your example inspires me daily to not only be a better rabbi but to be a better person.

To Jim and Nancy Holland, since the tenth grade you have been editing my writing with a close eye. I continue to learn great grammar from you, and, more importantly, great lessons for life.

To Alan Castel, thank you for teaching me neuroscience standing on one foot. I can't wait to read your first book.

To Lori Lepler, without your sage guidance this book would have never come to fruition. Thank you for helping me refine my vision for this book and for my life.

To Merrill Sparago and Kaye Michaelson, you never tire of listening to me even when I tire of myself. You are patient, understanding, and honest. Sometimes brutally. Thank you.

To Donna Lyons (aka Martha Stewart's younger sister), Sonia Chacon, and Amy Doyle, without you I could never fulfill my dreams of being a rabbi, mother, wife, daughter, author, and friend all on the same day. I hope I can show you the same kindness in return.

To Marcus and Rachelle Hirsch, with your quiet demeanor and Southern ways, you are one of my biggest fans. I celebrate you for modeling the true definition of "loyalty."

To Marlene Schwartz, you are a great aunt. I have discovered now why my mother called you every day for guidance. You are honest, caring, funny, and a good listener into the wee hours of the night.

To Emet, Eden, Alia, and Levi, each day the four of you refine my character, make me laugh, push me to my limits, and love me in ways I never could have imagined. Thank you for keeping me company in my office and in my life. I love being the cocaptain of Team Hirsch as my players rock! I love you to the moon and back.

To Jeff. You are a wonderful father and husband. In a short time we have crossed many thresholds together. Even though it has not always been easy, I'm so glad you are by my side.

To everyone who shares their stories with me in my office, in my classes, and on my retreats, thank you for your trust and your vulnerability. I am honored to hold you in my head and in my heart.

Finally I would like to thank those I hope to help in the writing of this book. You are my inspiration for always advancing to the next room.

Index